MORNING FOOD

Breakfasts, Brunches & More for Savoring the Best Part of the Day

Margaret S. Fox & John B. Bear
FOREWORD BY Alice Medrich
PHOTOGRAPHY BY Laurie Smith

TEN SPEED PRESS
Berkeley | Toronto

Dedication

To Stephanie Kroninger and Barbara Tropp,
cherished friends who died of cancer. Their spirits
continue to inspire me. I miss them every day.

Copyright © 1990, 2006 by Margaret S. Fox.

Text copyright © 1990, 2006 by John B. Bear and
Margaret S. Fox. All rights reserved.
Photography copyright © 2006 by Laurie Smith.

No part of this book may be reproduced in any form,
except for brief excerpts for the purpose of reviews,
without the written permission of the publisher.

1⊜

Ten Speed Press
PO Box 7123
Berkeley, California 94707
www.tenspeed.com

Distributed in Australia by Simon and Schuster
Australia, in Canada by Ten Speed Canada, in New
Zealand by Southern Publishers Group, in South
Africa by Real Books, and in the United Kingdom
and Europe by Publishers Group UK.

Library of Congress Cataloging-in-Publication Data
on file with the publisher.

ISBN-13: 978-1-58008-782-7
ISBN-10: 1-58008-782-5

Cover and text design by Betsy Stromberg
Photographs styled by Erica McNeish

The recipe and notes for China Moon Shanghai Rice,
copyright © 1989 by Barbara Tropp.

Printed in China

First printing, 2006
1 2 3 4 5 6 7 8 9 10 — 10 09 08 07 06

ACKNOWLEDGMENTS

I have the good fortune to call some pretty amazing people my friends. For their much-appreciated support, insight, love, kindness, and trustworthiness, my heartfelt thanks go to: Anne and Harold Fox, my very smart parents; Emily Fox, my wise and witty sister; and Celeste, my adorable daughter. Anne and Emily Fox, busy though they are, didn't hesitate to edit the heck out of my manuscript and help me sound more articulate. Harold Fox, the world's best salesman, started to promote this book even before I began the revision. His enthusiasm kept me going when I was overwhelmed.

Those as close as family include: Hilde and David Burton, Stephen Burton, Kathryn Wentzel, Sally Shepard, Howard Knight, Jeffery Garcia, Wendy and Jim Ponts, Sallie McConnell, Sara O'Donnell, Rick Steele, and Andy Semons. They have all contributed to my life in profound ways.

A big thank you to Steve and Ashley Jenks who cared about Cafe Beaujolais enough to buy it in 2000.

When I needed help with this project, Jocelyn Kamstra Sugrue stepped in with good humor and tested a great many recipes. And to all those who contributed recipes and stories, I appreciate your generosity. To the tasters, who graciously accepted even the less successful experiments, thanks!

Antonia Allegra enthusiastically encouraged me and my (ad)ventures and writing.

The multitalented Michael Carroll, a superb business coach and furniture maker, created the spreadsheet that made this entire project manageable.

Linda Carucci mentored me in significant ways without even realizing it because that's the kind of person she is.

Tom and Penny Honer welcomed me into the Harvest Market family, which has opened up a new world for me.

Caspar Children's Garden, Jessica Morton, Kathi Griffen, Deena Zarlin, Debra Castle, and Peg Brown-Levy have taken extremely good care of my daughter over the years.

John Bear, who appears in my life from time to time and matter-of-factly shows me that anything is possible, did it again.

And I am grateful to two of the greatest TV shows of all time—*Rocky and Bullwinkle* and *The Dick Van Dyke Show*—for their indelible influence on my young and impressionable sense of humor.

CONTENTS

A few words about Morning Food vi

Foreword 1

Introduction 2

Cereals & Fruit
4

Muffins, Cookies & Biscuits
16

Breads & Scones
28

Coffee Cakes
48

Pancakes, Waffles,
French Toast & Crêpes
60

Eggs
80

Sandwiches & Soups
104

Side Dishes & Salads
118

Spreads, Sauces
& Dressings
132

Entrées
146

Desserts
162

Drinks
190

Index 197

A few words about
Morning Food

Thousands of restaurants across the country serve "breakfast all day." But typical lunch and dinner items, such as sandwiches, soups, and desserts, rarely appear on breakfast menus. Thus, convention dictates that if you want meat in the morning, your options are Eggs Benedict or the Lumberjack Special. Ice cream with a short stack or a burrito with an omelette? Probably not. Pizza, pasta, or polenta as a breakfast entrée? I don't think so. Pumpkin pie or chocolate cake before twelve? Are you kidding?

Cafe Beaujolais, in the tiny village of Mendocino, 160 coastal miles north of San Francisco, was beloved by local patrons and national reviewers alike, who tried for years to figure out what made breakfast at the Cafe so very special. At least part of the answer was that we *didn't* serve breakfast, we served *Morning Food.*

We took ingredients that most of us associate with the comfort and conventions of breakfast and shaped them into dozens of wonderful specialties whose only common denominator was that they were utterly delicious—and they were served in the morning. The Morning Food philosophy gave our patrons permission to indulge in a wide array of splendid dishes, without guilt or embarrassment, before the sun was high in the sky.

Decades later, this gently subversive approach to dining continues to ensure that you won't have to rationalize anything you choose to put in your mouth before noon. However, if you wish to justify an unusual choice, simply point out that the ingredients are standard breakfast classics that have been used in creative combinations. For example, instead of corn flakes and toast, keep the corn and the bread, add a few spices, and transform it into Tex-Mex Corn Bread Pudding.

Of course, there is more to the Morning Food ideal than just rearranging ingredients in interesting ways. Indeed, much of it *is* traditional breakfast and brunch fare: omelettes, eggs, pastries, and pancakes. But there is a level of care taken with each dish that Cafe Beaujolais customers, as well as fans of the first edition of *Morning Food,* found both satisfying and nurturing. It is my hope that the new edition of *Morning Food* lives up to the expectations of all those legions of happy diners and readers and that a new generation of Morning Food disciples is born.

FOREWORD

I first met Margaret Fox over the phone almost thirty years ago. At the time, Cocolat, my fledgling chocolate dessert shop in North Berkeley, was going gangbusters. Margaret called for some advice about which chocolate would be best for something she was baking for a shop in Mendocino, 150 miles to the north. I remember discussing whether or not one could legally sell a product that was, er, uh, made at home. We felt instantly familiar and comfortable with each other, and so began a life-long friendship.

To thank me for whatever pearls of wisdom I might have bestowed that day, Margaret sent her version of a mediaeval Italian confection called *panforte*. She says I called back right away and said "I don't know what this is, but send 50 pounds of it!" We sold tons of it at Cocolat over the next several years. Always a whirlwind of creative energy, Margaret kept coming up with new flavors and new ways of packaging and marketing what was eventually christened Panforte di Mendocino.

Not long after our first chat, Margaret bought Cafe Beaujolais and although we seldom saw one another, I always felt I had a kindred spirit in Mendocino. And like so many others, I gained an intimate view of her enormous character and talent through her books, her recipes (which I still use), and her stories, told with that remarkable writer's voice—pure Margaret—which I so admire.

Margaret and I still don't see a lot of each other, but after thirty years of "doing something" with food, as Margaret would say, and being women, we've piled up an astonishing amount of shared experience. Talking (mostly via email) is still a pleasure and often inspiring; advice is freely given in both directions. Margaret is still a whirlwind of creativity and enthusiasm when she gets excited about something, as indeed she is, once again, on the topic of Morning Food.

Alice Medrich, author of *Bittersweet*
Berkeley, California

Introduction

For several years after I sold Cafe Beaujolais in 2000, people regularly approached me with the statement, "You must miss the restaurant." I shocked them by saying, "No, I don't." How could a business that was my life for 23 years, 2 months, and a day not leave a gaping hole once I had let go of it? I think because I was ready. Yes, I loved it, I loved the staff, I loved the customers, and I loved the garden and the Brickery. But I was also tired, bone-weary tired, of this incredibly demanding business. And yet when I returned to the civilian life I thought I so desired, the contrast stunned me. Who knew that "real" life could seem so strange?

You may be wondering, "What is she talking about?" For starters, there is the *relentless* meal planning, shopping, cooking, cleaning up. So much work for a mere household? On the rare occasions when home-cooking happened during my Beaujolais years, provisions were assembled after a quick trip to the restaurant's walk-in refrigerator, laden with superb organic ingredients. I used to joke that I'd never leave the restaurant business because washing dishes at home was so tedious. But it wasn't so funny when I turned out to be right.

The real shocker was cooking for my daughter Celeste, who turned out to be the most demanding customer of my life. An adventuresome eater when she was very young, she narrowed her food choices drastically for several years. Too many nights of plain boiled noodles with Parmesan cheese followed, while my lovingly prepared "Mama food" (her words) was callously pushed aside.

The cost of eating in "real" life also stunned me. Every day for nearly a quarter of a century, I had most of my meals at the restaurant. Of course, I was well aware of those expenses (costs were scrutinized regularly), but it's different when the money comes out of your own pocket. Factor in that I also worked more waking hours than the average couple combined, and it's amazing how little money you spend when you don't have time to do anything else but work.

Perhaps other restaurateurs lead lives more balanced and integrated than mine, but I doubt it. I recall a gourmet magazine feature profiling the contents of a chef's home refrigerator. What was revealed was a sorry assortment of sour milk, moldy cheese, and a flaccid carrot to round out the food groups. I read that article, ruefully, recognizing a kindred soul.

Although much has already been written about the restaurant business, a veil of glamour still screens the less-exciting realities from public view. Or perhaps it's hard to believe just how taxing a business it is: the endless hours of standing, the heavy lifting, the intense heat, the stress, the interpersonal complexities, the less-than-ideal diet. And did I mention the heat? And the stress? Now I understand why one of my close relatives burst into tears and sobbed, "For *this* you went to college?" when I told her, in 1977, that I had bought a restaurant.

It took about three years without Cafe Beaujolais in my life to create balance in what I think of as my "recovery phase." And this brings me to this book and its origin. Why a revision of recipes from a restaurant I no longer own?

In November 2003, I attended the Women Chefs and Restaurateurs' 10th annual conference. (You can take the girl out of the restaurant, but not the restaurant out of the girl.) To my amazement, I was approached several times by women from all over the country who told me how influential my books had been: they quoted my text, they cited my recipes, they recalled experiences I had written about that had affected their career decisions. I was astonished. My only intention had been to inspire readers to head for the kitchen and prepare a good meal. Evidently, I had done more than I knew.

John Bear, my co-author, and I discussed this, and he suggested we write a new edition of *Morning Food*. A review of the recipes revealed that oat bran, for example, apparently deemed an essential ingredient in the early 1980s, does *not* enhance all baked goods. And recipe yields have been changed to reflect a more restrained, but no less enthusiastic, approach to rich foods.

Working on the new edition has brought back what I loved most about those years at Cafe Beaujolais but happily now have in my own home:

getting up early and "going to work" in my sun-drenched kitchen, filling the house with delicious smells, and feeding hungry friends who just happen to drop by when another coffee cake is coming out of the oven. These activities have put me back in touch with the very best parts of my "old" life.

I still live in Mendocino, but nowadays I work in Fort Bragg at a job that I love as Culinary Director of the vibrant and exciting Harvest Market, the world's largest (40,000-square-foot) pantry. And I look forward to seeing my products in Harvest at Mendosa's in Mendocino.

Nowadays a gym bag holding my daughter's soccer uniform sits on the counter next to my professional mixer. This juxtaposition sums up my "new" life. What more could anyone want?

Margaret Fox
Mendocino, California
morningfood@margaretfox.com

CEREALS & FRUIT

Margaret's Muesli
6

Birchard Soaked Oats
8

Emily's Northeastern
Breakfast Treat
9

Caramelized Applesauce
10

Fried Bananas
11

Past-Its-Prime Poached Fruit
à la Mom
12

Poached Apples & Pears
with Crème Fraîche
13

Rhubarb Glop
14

Sausage-Stuffed Baked Apples
15

Margaret's Muesli

Makes about 2¹/₂ cups

This healthy cereal originated in Europe, and I enjoyed it mornings when I lived in Austria. Some variations have more sugar in them than I like. If this version isn't sweet enough for you, add the optional sweetening. I like muesli stirred into yogurt, but it is also delicious with milk or apple juice.

1 cup toasted oats

3 tablespoons toasted wheat germ

3 tablespoons ground flax seeds

¹/₂ cup dried fruit, cut into small pieces: raisins, apricots, or prunes

¹/₂ cup lightly toasted nuts: hazelnuts, walnuts, or almonds

Yogurt, milk, or apple juice

Maple syrup, honey, or brown sugar

Mix together everything except the sweetening, adding as desired.

To toast the oats: Spread rolled oats in a thin layer in a baking pan. Bake at 350°F for about 15 minutes, until lightly toasted. Stir once or twice while baking.

Where Do New Recipes Come From?

It really helps to have an ability for "mental" tasting. Musicians can look at a score and hear the music in their heads. It's the same way with recipes for me. I look at the list of ingredients and can reflect on whether this flavor will go with that flavor, and how it will all taste. (I think I developed this skill because there were always so many cookbooks around our house when I was a kid, and I used to read them for pleasure, imagining how things would taste.)

Mental tasting used to come into play in real life when I went into the walk-in refrigerator at the restaurant. Faced with the challenge of 147 potential ingredients, I would think, "Oh, there are tomatoes, and there's some feta, and there are some olives, and some cilantro—what else sounds good? Lemons. Grated lemon peel, perhaps, for zing. What about the capers? No, too much." And suddenly there was an omelette filling.

Birchard Soaked Oats

Makes 1 serving

No one can eat rich or rich-tasting food *all* the time. I observed that Cafe Beaujolais customers who came in four or five or six days (or meals) in a row would, somewhere along the way, switch to a lighter food choice such as waffles with fruit, or granola, or these wholesome oats soaked in apple juice. Perhaps to cleanse the palate for another round of high living?

Mendocino residents and recipe contributors John and Barbara Birchard (he a former woodworker turned professional photographer; she a respected acupressure practitioner) had been restaurant regulars since the early days. One foggy morning they came in for breakfast with their baby. The place was empty except for the four of us, and I remember performing my "leaping frog" imitation (hopping around on the dining room floor), which none of the Birchards has held against me all these years.

1/3 cup uncooked rolled oats

1/4 cup apple juice

2 generous tablespoons yogurt, flavor of your choice

1 drop vanilla extract

1 tablespoon oat bran

1 heaping tablespoon coarsely chopped toasted almonds

1 heaping tablespoon raisins, or other similarly sized dried fruit

Fresh fruit, as desired: bananas, berries, or peaches

Soak the oats in the juice for 15 minutes, then add the remaining ingredients.

Emily's Northeastern Breakfast Treat

Makes 1 serving

When my younger sister Emily and I were little, we read a story about an unhappy girl who was sent to live with her strict grandparents in New England. One of her few pleasures was pouring hot, freshly boiled maple syrup onto the snow and eating it as a sticky candy, officially known in those parts as Sugar on Snow. To Californians born-and-raised, who had not yet traveled much, tales of maple syrup actually coming from sap out of *trees* seemed wondrous indeed.

My sister lives all too far away on the East Coast in Western Massachusetts, where she has actually participated in the following exotic event. She assures me that the finished dish is not sickeningly sweet but rather subtly so, because pre-boiled sap has the substance of water with but a whisper of sweetness. Did you know that 40 gallons of sap boil down to 1 gallon of maple syrup? I realize that many readers will not be able to make this dish because of geographical limitations, but now you have something splendid to look forward to, as do I.

1 maple tree with sap rising

1 friend who taps maple trees

Oats, cracked wheat, or other favorite cereal

Butter

Milk

Wait until late winter or early spring.

Tap your maple tree and obtain 1 quart of fresh sap. Use as the liquid to cook the grain cereal of your choice. According to Emily, "...the resulting flavor, a rich blend of nutty grain and subtle sweetness, is extremely satisfying and requires nothing more than a little butter or milk. This is what Maypo would like to be when it grows up."

Caramelized Applesauce

Makes 4 to 5 cups

Once I had the pleasure of working with Gaston LeNôtre, perhaps France's premier pastry chef, at the Great Chefs of France Cooking School, held at the Robert Mondavi Winery. Everything Gaston did had a touch of magic about it. My chunky applesauce is inspired by his. It is delicious as a topping for blintzes or crêpes or rice pudding, or stirred into yogurt or cottage cheese.

About 4 1/2 pounds cooking apples (I use Granny Smith)

1 1/3 cups water

Juice of half a lemon

2 cups sugar

1/2 vanilla bean, split in half lengthwise

Peel and core the apples, and place peels and cores in a saucepan. Add water, bring to a boil, lower the heat, and simmer for 5 minutes. Cut each apple into 6 wedges, place in a bowl, and toss with lemon juice, coating every surface of each wedge.

Strain the cooking liquid from the peels and cores through a sieve over a large pan, pressing hard to extract as much liquid as possible. Add sugar to the liquid in the pan and bring slowly to a boil, stirring gently with a wooden spoon until the sugar melts. If any sugar sticks to the sides of the pan, remove it with a moistened pastry brush.

When the syrup comes to a boil, raise the heat and boil rapidly for 10 minutes until it reaches 313°F, stirring occasionally. As soon as the syrup begins to turn a caramel color, carefully add the apples and vanilla bean. *Be very careful to avoid splattering syrup as it is incredibly hot.*

Cook for 5 minutes, then lower the heat and cook at a slow boil for about 20 minutes, or until the apples begin to fall apart. The finished sauce should be chunky, not smooth. Please don't stir the apples; instead, simply shake the pan gently.

Fried Bananas

Makes 1 serving or, conceivably, 2

A recipe straight from the headquarters of Lily-Gilders, Inc. (My mother and I are officers of this organization whose mission is to make every meal, no matter how good, just a little bit better.) You start with one basic banana and, by the time you are done, you have something that looks spectacular and tastes divine. There is no limit to the amount of gilding you are hereby given permission to do on this particular banana-lily. The only caution is to move quickly while you are making it.

Fried Bananas are delicious on their own, on ice cream, or as a wonderful topping for pancakes and waffles.

1 medium banana, green-tipped

1 tablespoon butter

2 to 3 teaspoons lemon or lime juice

1 tablespoon brown sugar, maple syrup, or honey

2 tablespoons dark rum or brandy

Optional lily-gilding extras: cinnamon, nutmeg, toasted walnuts, sesame seeds, coconut, yogurt, sour cream, and/or ice cream

Peel the banana and cut it lengthwise, then crosswise, making 4 pieces. Melt the butter in a small frying pan and brown the banana pieces *quickly* on both sides, about 2 minutes at most. Mix together the juice and sweetening and pour over bananas. Turn the bananas to coat both sides as the syrup bubbles and thickens. Heat the rum or brandy, pour it over bananas, and present it all on fire. Serve with a wide spatula. Pour the possibly-still-flaming sauce over. Garnish with any or all of the optional ingredients.

Past-Its-Prime Poached Fruit à la Mom

Makes 4 to 6 servings

At one time or another, we've all bought fruit that looks perfect in the store, only to get home, take a bite of it, and say, "Blecchhh." When this happened to my frugal mom, she devised this recipe, which is a clever way of making something end up much better than one might have expected at the start. Although she is normally a recipe-oriented cook, this preparation can be quite spontaneous, so I hovered at her elbow, paper and pen in hand, as she tossed "a little of this" and "a little of that" into the pan.

Of course, the recipe works perfectly well with fruit that's in season, but it's hardly needed. You could use cotton balls, and it would probably turn out swell. If you use more than one type of fruit, you may wish to re-title the recipe Poached Fruit Mélange. Use only fruit that has stones or pits or seeds: apples, peaches, pears, apricot, plums. It doesn't work with soft fruits, such as strawberries, bananas, or pineapples.

The perfumed light syrup created during cooking demands fresh, whole spices. Don't let your fragile spices sit in the cupboard for years and years as the flavor will slowly disappear and your dishes will end up tasteless.

You might experiment with other wines, as well. Gewürztraminer makes this equally delicious, but quite different. Mom has even used jug wine. Whatever you use, you'll almost certainly come out with something that is better than the sum of its parts.

1 cup vermouth or dry white wine

1 cup water

1/2 cup white sugar

1 cinnamon stick, about 3 inches long

6 whole cloves

15 cardamom seeds, removed from their whitish pods

3 whole allspice berries

1/4 teaspoon anise seed

Juice of half a lemon, about 2 tablespoons

Fruit past-its-prime: 4 pears, cored and peeled if you wish, and cut into quarters or slices, or an equivalent quantity of peaches, apples, apricots, or plums

Place all the ingredients, except the fruit, into a large pot and simmer, uncovered, for about 5 minutes. Slice the fruit any way you wish. Twelve slices for each pear make an attractive presentation. Add fruit, bring to a boil, cover, and reduce the heat. Simmer for about 3 to 5 minutes, or until fruit is tender. Cooking time depends on ripeness and the size of the fruit slices, so check the fruit with a sharp knife to see if it is tender. When done, remove from heat and let cool.

Refrigerate for at least 8 hours before serving. Sometimes my mom adds 1 cup of blueberries or other berries after the fruit is removed from the heat.

Poached Apples & Pears with Crème Fraîche

Makes 4 to 6 servings

Here is a fresh fruit compote that you can make pretty much all year round, or at least as long as pears are available. You can make it the day before, and refrigerate it overnight. It can be served as an appetizer, or as the fruit accompaniment to an egg dish. Served over cottage cheese, it becomes the main event of the meal.

I feel that cutting back on sugar is more important to the diet than many other so-called healthy things we do. And the natural sweetness of the fruit and the honey make this dish plenty sweet enough. It doesn't need to be quite this rich; in fact, the crème fraîche can be replaced with drained yogurt, if you prefer.

The white wine is a nice addition because it balances all the flavors and refreshes your palate. Food that is entirely sweet or entirely tart is boring. I eat two bites and suddenly I've had enough of *that*.

Pears out of season may seem to be too hard, but no worries—poaching will render them pleasantly juicy.

3 apples

3 pears, preferably ripe, but not
    mushy

2$^1/_4$ cups apple juice

1 cup dry white wine

2 tablespoons honey

1 cinnamon stick

$^1/_4$ teaspoon nutmeg

Zest of 1 lemon and 1 orange,
    finely chopped

$^1/_2$ cup Crème Fraîche (page 135)

$^1/_4$ teaspoon powdered cinnamon

Peel and core the apples and slice each into about 10 pieces. Peel and core the pears and slice each into about 8 pieces.

Put the apple juice, wine, honey, cinnamon stick, and nutmeg in a large pot and bring to a boil. Reduce the heat and simmer for 10 minutes. Add the apple slices and citrus zest and simmer for about 5 minutes, until apples are almost tender. Add the pear slices and poach for 3 minutes.

Pour into a bowl, cover, and refrigerate overnight. Serve with a dollop of crème fraîche and a dusting of powdered cinnamon.

Rhubarb Glop

Makes about 1 quart

I think rhubarb is one of America's great underrated fruits or vegetables or weeds or whatever it is. Poor rhubarb has led a tortured life: most of us, if we do anything at all with it, stew it with half a ton of sugar. Believe me, it deserves a better fate.

My mom did the definitive research to demonstrate that rhubarb does *not* require immense amounts of sugar. One summer, she made batch after batch of stewed rhubarb, each one with a little less sugar than the last. By August, very little sugar was required. Of course it was tart, but in quite a pleasant way.

This particular glop isn't exactly light on sugar, but one doesn't serve a whole lot of glop at one time. It appears, for instance, as a relish for the Smoked Turkey Salad Sandwich (page 109). And it becomes the base of the Strawberry-Rhubarb Pie (page 174), which has no added sugar at all. I wouldn't want to eat this all by itself, but I have eaten it as a stand-alone dish, supplemented with plain yogurt, which mellows it nicely. It will keep in the refrigerator for up to six weeks, and it freezes well.

3 pounds rhubarb
2¹/₄ cups sugar
3 tablespoons grated fresh ginger
6 tablespoons lemon juice

Remove the rhubarb leaves and wash the stalks. Cut the rhubarb into ¹/₂-inch chunks. In a large bowl, mix with sugar and cover with plastic wrap. Place in the refrigerator overnight.

Stir the mixture well, scraping the bowl to incorporate any undissolved sugar, then place in a colander and drain directly into a saucepan. Place the rhubarb back in the bowl and bring the syrup in the pan to a boil. When all the sugar is dissolved, pour the syrup back over the rhubarb, stir, and let sit 15 minutes.

Drain through a sieve. Measure 1 cup of the syrup and return to a pot large enough to hold all the rhubarb too. (Save the rest of the syrup to make Rhubarb Syrup, page 195.)

Add the rhubarb, ginger, and lemon juice, stir, and cook over medium heat, stirring frequently, until the rhubarb is soft, but not mushy. Let cool, and refrigerate.

Sausage-Stuffed Baked Apples

Makes 4 servings

Someone was recounting a recipe for baked apples and said, "Of course, you cover the apples up, because you know how ugly they are." I replied that baked apples aren't ugly, they're homely. The wait staff at Cafe Beaujolais sometimes asked "Oh, what happened to those apples?" Nothing happened, darn it. That's the way they're *supposed* to look.

This recipe is both homely and unusual because it combines sweet and savory flavors. It can be a meal in itself or an accompaniment to waffles, pancakes, eggs, or French toast, the usual breakfast suspects. The sweetness comes from the apple and the apple juice concentrate.

Use chicken-apple sausage that is light and delicate, preferably something you can obtain freshly made. Note: The apple is not merely cored; it is hollowed out to create a larger space to hold the filling.

4 baking apples, similar in size (I use Rome Beauty or Golden Delicious)

1 tablespoon butter

1 cup minced yellow onions

1/3 cup finely chopped celery

1/4 cup currants

2 teaspoons freshly and finely grated ginger

2/3 cup undiluted apple juice concentrate, straight from the can

4 ounces chicken-apple sausage

Preheat the oven to 275°F.

Core the apples, leaving the bottom stem intact to allow the apple to hold the filling securely. Enlarge the hole with a small knife to create a space about 2 inches deep and 2 inches across. Be sure the apple "wall" is at least half an inch thick. Peel the outside of each apple about halfway down. Chop up the apple "insides" and set aside.

Melt the butter over medium heat in a large skillet and add the onions. Sauté for about 5 minutes, then add the celery and apple insides and continue cooking for another 5 minutes until soft. Add the currants, ginger, and 1/4 cup of the apple juice concentrate, and bring to a boil. Cook over high heat for about 30 seconds, until the liquid starts to thicken. Set aside.

Sauté the sliced or crumbled sausage until browned and add to apple mixture. Stir to combine.

Divide mixture among the four apples and place them in an 8- by 8-inch pan. Mix the remaining apple juice concentrate with 2 cups water and pour in the bottom of the pan.

Bake for about 1 to 1½ hours. Baste the apples generously with the liquid several times during baking. If the tops start to brown, cover them with foil. Test apples with a knife. When it goes in easily (no crunch), they're done. Let sit at room temperature until warm, then serve. Or let cool, then refrigerate. Cover the whole apple in foil and reheat to serve.

MUFFINS, COOKIES & BISCUITS

Bran Muffins
18

Oatmeal-Raisin Muffins
19

Name That Muffin
20

Applesauce-Raisin-Nut Muffins
21

Stinson Beach
Blueberry Muffins
22

Mocha Walnut
Wonder Muffins
24

Morning Glory Muffins
25

Breakfast Cookies
26

Cornmeal Biscuits
on the Square
27

Bran Muffins

Makes 1 dozen muffins

The world may already be overwhelmed by bran muffins (or anything with oat bran) at this point, but this is a great little recipe. The coffee in the batter makes it unusual. When combined with the other ingredients, it doesn't taste like coffee, but does give the muffins a deeper, richer flavor. Also, I confess, it lures me into eating a little bit of the batter before it turns into muffins.

I cut back on the sugar because so many sweet things are just *too* sweet.

It is really important not to overbeat the batter. Just stir until blended. Overbeaten muffin batter results in ugly muffins, with funny looking tops and big gaping holes inside. I used to get neurotic about this in the restaurant, because we used a big powerful mixer and, if someone was distracted or just turned away even for just a moment, the batter got tough and there was no way to repair it.

1 large egg

1/3 cup brown sugar

1/4 cup canola oil

1/2 cup strong coffee

1 cup buttermilk

1/2 teaspoon salt

2 1/4 cups white flour

1 1/4 teaspoons baking soda

3 tablespoons oat bran

1 1/2 cups bran cereal

*1/2 cup raisins, dried prunes, or
any other dried fruit*

Mix the egg, sugar, oil, coffee, buttermilk, and salt. Sift together the flour and baking soda, stir in the bran and bran cereal, and add this mixture to the liquid ingredients. Stir just until blended. Quickly stir in the raisins. Refrigerate the batter overnight. Scoop into prepared muffin tins and bake at 400°F for about 20 minutes.

Oatmeal-Raisin Muffins

Makes about 1 dozen muffins

This is probably the most widely distributed recipe I shall ever publish. It was prepared for the Pacific Gas and Electric Company's newsletter, and was mailed to untold millions of households along with their utility bill. If you were one of those recipients, I apologize for being redundant, but it is a fine little recipe for a fine little muffin. And I don't think you can ever have too many muffin recipes. These are especially nice when you're preparing an elaborate breakfast or brunch, because they are so fast and easy to make. The batter keeps well, so you can make it the night before.

1 cup rolled oats
1 cup buttermilk
³/4 cup white flour
¹/2 teaspoon baking powder
¹/4 teaspoon salt
³/4 teaspoon baking soda
¹/2 teaspoon cinnamon
2 large eggs, beaten lightly
¹/3 cup light brown sugar
6 tablespoons melted butter
¹/3 cup raisins

Combine the oats and buttermilk, and let stand 30 minutes.

Sift together the flour, baking powder, salt, baking soda, and cinnamon.

Stir the eggs into the buttermilk mixture, then add sugar, butter, and the flour mixture. Stir until just combined. The batter will be lumpy. Fold in the raisins.

Spoon into a muffin tin, filling the cups about two-thirds full. Bake at 400°F for 15 to 20 minutes.

Name That Muffin

Makes about 18 muffins

The personality of this muffin changes depending on the fruit or vegetable that is added to the batter. It has been a longtime favorite for two reasons: one, because the ginger adds an unexpected spiciness to the flavor; and two, when I have leftover bruised but still edible fruits or vegetables I'm dying to use up, this is where they go. So far, I've tried apples, pears, oranges, zucchini, tomatoes, plums, even fresh pumpkin. Keep experimenting.

One interesting option is to divide the batter into several batches and add different fruits or vegetables to each batch.

2 cups white flour

$3/4$ teaspoon salt

$3/4$ teaspoon baking soda

$1/4$ teaspoon baking powder

2 large eggs

$3/4$ cup brown sugar

$3/4$ cup canola oil

$3/4$ teaspoon vanilla extract

$1^1/3$ cups prepared fruit or vegetables

$1^1/2$ teaspoons cinnamon

$1^1/2$ teaspoons powdered ginger

$1/3$ cup poppy seeds

$3/4$ cup coarsely chopped toasted walnuts

Preheat oven to 400°F.

Sift together the flour, salt, baking soda, and baking powder. In a separate bowl, whip the eggs with the sugar and oil. Stir in the vanilla, whatever fruits or vegetables you are using, the spices, and the poppy seeds. Then add the flour mixture and the nuts. Please do not overmix.

Spoon the batter into greased or papered muffin cups, filling each about three-quarters full. Bake for 25 to 30 minutes, until golden brown.

Variation: Add apples or pears, cored and shredded.
Variation: Add unpeeled zucchini, shredded.
Variation: Add oranges, washed thoroughly, chopped (skin, pulp, and juice), and processed in a food processor. Then add $1/3$ cup extra poppy seeds, 1 extra teaspoon ginger, and $1/2$ extra teaspoon cinnamon.
Variation: Add fresh pumpkin, steamed and chopped into small pieces.
Variation: Add tomatoes, chopped into small pieces.

Applesauce-Raisin-Nut Muffins

Makes about 20 muffins

The ton of apples our innocent-looking orchard yielded (no exaggeration) motivated us to create recipes of every description. For a while, we made richly flavored apple butter from little-known heirloom varieties, such as Rhode Island Greening, Tomkins King, Winter Banana, and Baldwin. (In case you are wondering, Winter Banana is not an apple with an identity crisis.) Originally, this recipe was made with apple butter, but since you probably don't have the same out-of-control apple problem we did, you can use applesauce, a less complicated preparation.

Be careful to mix the ingredients just enough to combine the wet with the dry. In the restaurant's recipe file, the recipe was annotated, in big yellow letters:

Urgent message: Do not overmix or Margaret will have a nervous breakdown. This is because muffins are fairly fragile and are adversely affected by too much beating. Little did my 8th-grade Home-Ec teacher, Mrs. Lamson, know how impressed I would still be, years later, by the photos of muffins cut in half, revealing a variety of terminal muffin ailments—cavernous holes and a tough texture due to overmixing, flattened tops from old leavening, extreme paleness or darkness from an uncalibrated oven. The moral of this tale is to mix just enough and use a reliable oven thermometer (and pay attention to Mrs. Lamson).

2 large eggs

1 1/2 cups applesauce

1/3 cup canola oil

1/3 cup brown sugar

1/3 cup white sugar

2 1/4 cups white flour

1 tablespoon baking powder

1/2 teaspoon baking soda

1 teaspoon salt

3/4 teaspoon cinnamon

1/2 teaspoon freshly ground nutmeg

2/3 cup raisins

1 cup coarsely chopped toasted walnuts

Preheat oven to 375°F.

Combine the eggs, applesauce, oil, and sugars.

In a separate bowl, sift together the flour, baking powder, baking soda, salt, cinnamon, and nutmeg. Add dry ingredients to wet, sprinkle the raisins and walnuts over the flour mixture, and stir just until mixed.

Pour batter into muffin tins prepared with papers or nonstick spray, and bake for 20 to 25 minutes, until a deep golden brown.

Stinson Beach Blueberry Muffins

Makes 20 muffins

These sublime crunchy-topped muffins came to me from my talented friend Leslie Martin, who collected the blueberries one beautiful afternoon at Stinson Beach north of San Francisco. Leslie, a former travel editor with a Doctorate in French studies, recently completed an account of her life with a peasant family in a village in the Dordogne.

2 large eggs
1/2 cup brown sugar
1/2 cup canola oil
1 cup heavy whipping cream
1 1/2 teaspoons vanilla extract
1/4 teaspoon ground nutmeg
1 cup white flour
1 cup whole-wheat flour
Pinch of salt
1 tablespoon baking powder
1 cup chopped toasted almonds
1 cup fresh frozen blueberries

Preheat oven to 400°F.

In a large bowl, mix together the eggs, sugar, oil, cream, and vanilla. Set aside.

In another bowl, sift together the nutmeg, flours, salt, and baking powder. Add the egg mixture to the flour bowl and stir quickly—just enough to blend ingredients—for about 15 to 20 seconds.

Fold in the almonds and frozen berries and pour into muffin tins prepared either with papers or nonstick spray. Bake for 18 to 20 minutes, until golden.

No One Wants a Bleeding Berry

When using fresh berries in a batter, it really helps if you freeze them first for at least an hour and a half beforehand. Then they don't bleed all over your batter as you stir them in. Even when the berries themselves are an attractive color, be prepared for the batter to turn a less-than-lovely hue. For instance, the deep ultramarine of blueberries turns batter a pallid gray when cooked.

Mocha Walnut Wonder Muffins

Makes about 16 muffins

This may be the first and only cookbook to mention Robert Redford and Stevie Wonder (although not in the same recipe). Anni Amberger is a professional party planner who also specializes in one-of-a-kind edible art pieces, like the heart-shaped chocolate cake topped with a portrait of Frida Kahlo created in marzipan. Many years ago, Anni worked in Oakland at a small café frequented by musicians. One day, she heard that Stevie Wonder was coming in, so she invented these muffins in his honor. They were a grand success, and he took a batch of them home.

I have added a bit more chocolate to her original recipe. If there is going to be *any* chocolate in a muffin, I really want to know it's there. The chocolate chips make it more of a cupcake than a muffin, but you can eat it at any time of the day.

3 large eggs

3/4 cup canola oil

1 cup buttermilk

1/2 cup strong black coffee

1 teaspoon vanilla extract

1/3 cup cocoa (sifted, then measured)

1 1/2 cups white flour

1 1/4 cups whole wheat flour

1 cup firmly packed brown sugar

1/2 teaspoon baking powder

1 teaspoon baking soda

1 teaspoon salt

1 cup chopped walnuts

1 cup semisweet chocolate chips

Preheat oven to 375°F.

Combine the eggs, oil, buttermilk, coffee, and vanilla, and set aside.

Sift the rest of the ingredients, except for the nuts and chocolate chips, into a separate bowl. Add the nuts and chocolate chips, and stir. Add the dry mixture to the wet and mix quickly, just until blended. Please do not dawdle and do not overmix.

Spoon the batter into prepared muffin tins and bake for about 20 to 25 minutes, or until done. Test with a toothpick inserted into the center of the muffin. When it comes out clean, the muffins are done.

Morning Glory Muffins

Makes 24 to 28 muffins

These sweet morsels taste rather like carrot cake in muffin form.

2^1/4 cups white flour

1^1/3 cups sugar

2 teaspoons baking powder

2 teaspoons baking soda

2 teaspoons salt

1 tablespoon cinnamon

3 cups (about ^{1}/2 pound) grated
 carrots

2 cups (about 6 ounces) grated
 apples

1^1/4 cups shredded sweetened
 coconut

1 cup chopped toasted pecans

^{3}/4 cup raisins

4 large eggs

^{3}/4 cup canola oil

2 teaspoons vanilla extract

Preheat oven to 375°F.

Sift together the flour, sugar, baking powder, baking soda, salt, and cinnamon. Set aside.

In a large bowl, mix together the carrots, apple, coconut, pecans, and raisins. Add the eggs, oil, and vanilla; stir to combine. Stir in the flour mixture, just until blended. Please do not overbeat.

Scoop into muffin tins lined with papers and bake for 20 to 25 minutes, until done.

Breakfast Cookies

Makes about 6 dozen cookies

Cookies for breakfast? Okay, maybe they aren't the healthiest things to eat first thing in the morning, but you have to admit, all of these ingredients have been on your breakfast table at one time or another. If the Grape-Nuts cereal makes the cookies too crunchy for you, substitute a crunchy flake cereal.

1/2 cup unsalted butter, softened

1 cup firmly packed dark brown sugar

2 large eggs

3/4 cup canola oil

2 teaspoons vanilla extract

1 cup Grape-Nuts cereal

1/2 cup peanut butter

2 1/4 cups white flour

1 teaspoon baking powder

1 teaspoon baking soda

3/4 teaspoon salt

2 tablespoons wheat germ

2 tablespoons ground flax seeds

1/3 cup nonfat dry milk powder

1 cup raisins

Preheat oven to 350°F.

Cream together the butter and sugar. Add the eggs, oil, and vanilla, and mix to blend. Stir in the remaining ingredients.

Form dough into balls 1 inch in diameter. Place on ungreased 10- by 15-inch cookie sheets and flatten with a fork. Bake for about 12 minutes on a baking rack positioned in the middle of the oven. Remove from oven and let cool.

Cornmeal Biscuits on the Square

Makes 16 biscuits

These are not your conventional biscuits. Although they're made the same way as ordinary biscuits (which means they are fast and simple—the sort of thing you can do in the morning and serve them fresh and hot) they have more texture than buttermilk biscuits.

I gave up making round biscuits during my restaurant years. Since you're not supposed to touch the dough too much, why labor over a shape that requires so much handling? Not to mention the fact that you end up with all those little bits and pieces and lopped-off corners. Furthermore, the second batch of biscuits, made from the scraps left over from cutting round ones, never seems to come out quite as good as the first.

Cornmeal complements a lot of different flavors. I would serve these biscuits with cheese, or with eggs and salsa, or an omelette filled with my Black Bean Chili (page 153). The corn gives them some additional pizzazz. The little bit of sugar, incidentally, is there to brown the biscuits rather than to sweeten them. That's one of the chemical roles that sugar plays.

$1^3/4$ cups white flour

1 tablespoon white sugar

$1/4$ cup cornmeal

$2^1/2$ teaspoons baking powder

$1/4$ teaspoon baking soda

$3/4$ teaspoon salt

$1/3$ cup unsalted butter, cut into $1/2$-teaspoon-sized pieces, and frozen

$1/2$ cup buttermilk beaten with 1 large egg

Preheat oven to 425°F.

Place all the dry ingredients in a food processor. Blend. Add the butter and process for a few seconds (8 to 10 is all it takes) until the mixture is the texture of coarse meal. Quickly add the buttermilk and egg and process for about 4 seconds, just until dough forms.

Turn out onto a lightly floured board and knead about 5 times.

Roll out to a $3/4$-inch thickness, keeping the shape as square as possible (about 7 inches square) for attractive, uniform biscuits.

Cut into 16 pieces, place on an ungreased baking sheet, and bake for about 15 minutes, until brown on top and bottom.

Breads & Scones

Basic Sweet Roll Dough
30

Cinnamon Rolls
32

Cinnamon-Raisin Bread
33

Toasting Bread
34

Mandelbrot
36

Poppy Seed Yeast Bread
37

Bill Brown's Five-Flour
Brown Bread
38

Corn Bread
40

Jocelyn's Orange-Currant Scones
41

Polish Raisin Bread
42

Cindy's Cherry Chocolate-
Chip Scones
44

Basic Brioche Dough
45

Gramma Carroll's
Cinnamon Rolls
46

Basic Sweet Roll Dough

Makes 3¹/₄ pounds of dough

Food memories are the strangest things. Have you ever, as an adult, tasted something that you loved as a child, to find that it just doesn't taste all that good? A disheartening experience occurred with the original recipe for this dough—one that I fondly remembered from more than thirty years ago. How do I know it was so long ago? I was completely preoccupied in the kitchen as my mother was shouting, "Margaret, Margaret, come and watch; a man is walking on the moon." However, even that was not enough to make the original recipe merit inclusion here because the dough tasted so heavy and dull.

Five versions later, I finally arrived at the following recipe, which was a good thing, because my father had begun to dread yet another unsuccessful cinnamon roll. This basic dough has thousands of possible uses, among them Cinnamon Rolls (page 32), Cinnamon-Raisin Bread (page 33), and Almond- or Chocolate-filled Coffee Cake (page 57).

2 (2¹/₄-teaspoon) packets dry yeast (check expiration date)

¹/₄ cup warm water, 110°F

¹/₂ cup sugar

¹/₂ cup melted unsalted butter

1 tablespoon grated orange zest (optional)

³/₄ cup warm milk

¹/₂ cup instant nonfat dry milk powder

2 teaspoons salt

4 large eggs

About 5¹/₂ cups white flour

In a small bowl, dissolve the yeast in warm water with a pinch of the sugar. Stir and set in a warm place, about 80°F, until foamy, about 5 minutes.

In a 4-quart bowl, using a wooden spoon, mix together the rest of the sugar, the butter, optional orange peel, warm milk, dry milk powder, salt, eggs, 3 cups of flour, and the yeast mixture. Add 1 cup of flour and beat like crazy—that's *beat*, not *stir*— for about 5 minutes, until dough strands come away from the sides of the bowl. This is an indication that the gluten, which is essential to the production of springy dough with a fine crumb, is developing.

Gradually, add up to 1¹/₂ cups more of flour. Various conditions, such as the weather and the absorbency of the flour, will determine the quantity of flour you'll need, so don't do anything rash, like dumping in all the flour at once. When the dough starts to pull away from the sides of the bowl, turn it out onto a lightly floured board and knead, adding a little flour if it begins to stick. You must continue kneading the dough for 5 minutes after your final addition of flour. The goal is a smooth, unsticky round of dough with air bubbles under the surface.

Place the dough in a greased bowl and cover with a damp towel or plastic wrap. Let it rise in a warm place until it has about doubled in size, about 1¹/₂ hours. Don't worry if the time is more or less;

working with yeast is imprecise at best. When the dough has risen, punch it down. If you are not ready to proceed, cover, and let it rise again for about 1 hour. The second rising always takes less time and will produce a finer, more delicate crumb. Punch the dough down, turn it out, and knead a few times to release air bubbles.

The dough is now ready to be made into its final form. The recipe that follows, Cinnamon Rolls, is an example.

Proof Your Yeast

Fresh leavening is very active, while the older stuff starts to get tired and not perform as well as it used to (kind of like us). Don't rely on appearance—the old looks the same as the young (not like us). Check the date on the package. When in doubt, "proof" it (that is, test it) by adding 1 teaspoon to $1/4$ cup warm water (105 to 110°F) along with $1/4$ teaspoon white sugar and stirring to combine. Set in a warm place for 5 to 10 minutes. If it foams and bubbles within that time, it's still active. If not, discard it. This technique works for baking soda (add $1/4$ teaspoon to 1 teaspoon of vinegar or lemon juice), and for baking powder (add $1/2$ teaspoon to $1/4$ cup hot water).

Cinnamon Rolls

Makes about 12 rolls

These are big, generous cinnamon rolls with a lot of stuff in them. When items like this don't have enough filling, somehow I feel cheated. To those people who think there is *too* much filling, I can only remind them forcefully that these are cinnamon rolls, not Ry-Krisp. And if you'd like even *more* filling... well, these can be just as decadent as you can make them.

I like this powdered sugar glaze, but then I'm not such a fan of gloppy glazes. This amount seems to make the finished product look and taste good. But if gloppy is your style, then you can certainly make more of the glaze and ladle it on to your heart's content.

This recipe calls for half of the Basic Sweet Roll Dough (page 30). Of course, you can double it, or you might want to make one pan of these and one loaf of Cinnamon-Raisin Bread (opposite), or any other sweet dough recipe.

4 tablespoons melted butter

$1^2/3$ cups firmly packed brown sugar

$1^1/2$ tablespoons cinnamon

Half of the Basic Sweet Roll Dough (page 30)

1 cup raisins or currants

$3/4$ cup walnuts

Powdered Sugar Glaze

$1/2$ cup powdered sugar (measured, then sifted)

1 teaspoon softened butter

$1/8$ teaspoon vanilla or almond extract

About 1 tablespoon hot water

1 teaspoon corn syrup

Preheat the oven to 350°F.

In a bowl, mix together the butter, sugar, and cinnamon.

Roll out the dough to a 12- by 15-inch rectangle. Sprinkle sugar and cinnamon mixture evenly over the surface of the dough, making sure to go all the way out to the edges. Sprinkle the raisins and walnuts over the sugar and pat everything lightly into the dough. Starting from the narrow side, tightly roll the dough. If anything edible falls out, scoop it up and place it back on the dough.

Cut the roll into 12 slices and place in a greased 9- by 13-inch pan, cut side up. Push any surface raisins into the dough, otherwise they will burn and taste terrible. Cover the pan with a towel and let the rolls rise in a warm place until they are extremely light, about 1 hour.

Bake for about 35 minutes, or until richly browned. If you are planning to serve the rolls at once, mix together with a spoon all the ingredients for the Powdered Sugar Glaze and drizzle it over them. Or dust them with powdered sugar. Serve warm.

Cinnamon-Raisin Bread

Makes 1 loaf

Although I've owned a restaurant and have three cookbooks to my name, I don't have all the answers. The truth is, sometimes my bread dough unfurls as it is rising in the pan. For a recipe with filling, this creates a mess, and I have no sure-fire way of avoiding it. (If you do, please let me know.) But I say emphatically that the bread tastes just as good *un*furled as furled. So if yours unfurls, tell your houseguests that it took years to perfect this famous technique.

Cinnamon bread is delicious toasted, but use a toaster oven to avoid the inevitable burning of the raisins that fall into the toaster slot without chance of recovery.

Half of the Basic Sweet Roll Dough (page 30)

1 cup firmly packed brown sugar

1 tablespoon cinnamon

2 tablespoons melted unsalted butter

1 cup raisins

Lightly grease a 9- by 5-inch bread pan. Roll the dough out to a 12- by 15-inch rectangle. Mix together the sugar, cinnamon, and butter. Sprinkle the mixture evenly over the surface of the dough, making sure to go within 1/4 inch of the edges. Sprinkle the raisins over the surface and pat everything lightly into the dough.

Starting from the narrow end, roll up tightly. If the dough and/or filling is squishing out of the ends, stuff the flotsam back in with your fingers. Pinch the ends and the bottom seam so the dough seals as securely as possible. It won't be perfect (expect a little mess), but do the best you can. Place the loaf in the pan, seam side down, cover, and let rise in a warm place until very light, about 1 hour.

Place in a preheated 350°F oven and bake until richly browned, about 35 minutes. Then run a knife around the loaf and carefully turn it out. Cool on a rack placed over a pan to catch any dripping sugar.

Toasting Bread

Makes 2 loaves

I am often asked what influenced me, culinarily speaking, as I was growing up. Well, obviously, my family played a huge role in terms of influence and encouragement. Another significant factor was *Sunset* magazine, in which I often found intriguing and challenging recipes that were explained in such detail they were practically guaranteed to turn out well. This version is based on a recipe in a bread article that appeared in the March 1968 issue.

This bread has a nice crumb, with enough white flour to keep it light. The original inspiration was to make bread with cornmeal in it that, when toasted, would not crumble in the infuriating way corn bread often does.

Regardless of the tantalizing aroma when you remove the loaves from the oven, resist cutting them for at least 2 hours. When sliced too warm, the texture is gummy.

2 (2¹/₄-teaspoon) packets dry yeast (check expiration date)

2 cups warm water, 110°F

1 cup nonfat dry milk powder

2¹/₂ teaspoons salt

¹/₄ cup canola oil

¹/₂ cup honey

About 4 cups white flour

²/₃ cup cornmeal

³/₄ cup toasted wheat germ

¹/₄ cup ground flax seeds

1¹/₂ cups whole-wheat flour

Dissolve the yeast in ¹/₄ cup of the water and stir. Set aside for 5 minutes, until foamy.

In a large bowl, combine the foamy yeast mixture, remaining warm water, dry milk powder, salt, oil, honey, and 3¹/₂ cups of the white flour. Whisk vigorously for 5 minutes, scraping down the sides occasionally, until strands of dough start to pull away from the sides of the bowl. Scrape down the sides again, cover the bowl tightly with plastic wrap, and set aside in a warm place to rise and double, about 1 hour.

When the dough has doubled, stir it down with a heavy wooden spoon. Mix in the cornmeal, wheat germ, and flaxseed meal. Add the whole-wheat flour, and when the dough is too stiff to stir, turn out onto a lightly floured board. Knead in about ¹/₄ cup more white flour; the dough will still be sticky. Cover it with a dry towel, and let it rest for 5 minutes. Knead it some more, and if it seems still a little sticky and difficult to knead, hit it repeatedly with your fist. The dough needs to be "exercised" somehow, and hitting is a good alternate move. After the last addition of flour, another 5 minutes of kneading is required.

Place the dough in a large oiled bowl. Turn the dough so all sides are oiled. Cover the bowl, and let the dough rise in a warm place, about 85°F, until almost doubled, about 1¹/₂ hours. Punch the dough down, turn it out, knead it a few times to remove air bubbles, divide it in half with a knife, and shape it.

To shape the dough, use the cut side as the bottom of the loaf. Pat and press the sides so that when the dough is placed in a greased 8- by 4-inch pan, the ends of the dough touch the ends of the pan. If the piece of dough is too short, it won't fill the pan properly. Brush melted butter on the loaves and set aside in a warm place, 85°F, to rise until almost doubled, about 50 to 60 minutes.

Bake loaves in a preheated 350°F oven for about 25 minutes, or until bread is richly browned. Cover with foil if the top appears too brown. Turn out, and let cool on racks for at least 2 hours before cutting.

Hands Versus Machines

In bread making, nothing replaces the touch of hand kneading. This is essential to understanding exactly how the dough feels, looks, and changes at every stage of its development. So practice the "hands-on" approach before turning to your electronic four-stage, computer-controlled, self-contained bread-o-matic.

Mandelbrot

Makes 3 to 4 dozen slices

For those who do not want a hearty meal in the morning, Mandelbrot (which means "almond bread") and a cup of coffee or tea may be a good way to start the day. This recipe can be made with hazelnuts, in which case the name becomes Haselnussbrot. Nowadays it seems as if everybody and her sister is making this sort of confection and its Italian cousin, biscotti (which means "twice-baked"), a cookie that is baked first in a loaf form, then sliced, then baked again.

The American Dental Association encourages the dunking of Mandelbrot because it is so hard, teeth have been known to chip. Besides the obvious coffee or tea, try hot chocolate, chocolate sauce, or hot milk and honey for dunking.

This recipe is my mom's and the finished product will keep almost forever in an airtight container, and if well hidden.

3¹/₂ cups white flour

2 teaspoons baking powder

¹/₄ teaspoon salt

3 large eggs

1 cup sugar

¹/₂ cup canola oil

2 teaspoons vanilla extract

¹/₂ teaspoon almond extract

1 cup chopped toasted almonds or hazelnuts

Preheat the oven to 350°F.

Sift the flour with the baking powder and salt, and set aside.

Beat the eggs and add the sugar gradually, beating until the batter is thick. Add the oil, vanilla and almond extracts, then the dry ingredients and nuts. Stir to combine. Divide the dough into 3 equal portions.

Sprinkle flour onto a pastry board and knead one portion of the dough for 2 or 3 minutes, until smooth and not sticky. Add a little more flour, if needed.

Shape the dough into a loaf about 9 inches long, ³/₄ of an inch high, and 2¹/₂ inches wide. Traditionally, the loaf has a slightly arched or curved top. Place across the width of a greased 9- by 13-inch pan. Repeat with the 2 remaining portions of dough. Bake for 30 to 35 minutes.

Remove the pan from the oven but *do not turn off oven.* Immediately remove the loaves and, with a sharp knife, cut into diagonal slices no more than ¹/₂ an inch thick.

Place the slices on ungreased 10- by 15-inch cookie sheets, return to the oven, and bake for about 12 to 15 minutes, until golden brown. During the baking, turn the slices over when one side is brown. Remove from the oven and let cool in the pan.

Poppy Seed Yeast Bread

Makes 1 loaf that serves 8 to 10

I like poppy seeds a lot. My dad, whose parents were from Hungary, was always on the lookout for pastry he remembered from his childhood. When we were little, he often took my sister and me to ethnic bakeries to seek out Mohnkuchen or Mohnstrudel, traditional Eastern European poppy seed pastries. From 1996 to 2000 I lived part of each year in the little town of Brixlegg in Austria's Tyrolean region. A special treat was going to Bäckerei Sigwart to enjoy their Mohnstrudel with a cup of flavorful Austrian coffee.

Few people seem to make this sort of yeasted coffee cake nowadays, a pity because it is an immensely satisfying process and impresses the heck out of your friends.

Bread

2 (2^1/$_4$-teaspoon) packets dry
    yeast (check expiration date)

^{1}/$_4$ cup warm water, 110°F

^{1}/$_4$ cup warm milk

^{1}/$_2$ teaspoon salt

^{1}/$_4$ cup sugar

1 large egg

^{1}/$_4$ cup unsalted butter, at room
    temperature

3 cups white flour

Egg wash: 1 egg white beaten
    with 1 teaspoon water

3 tablespoons sliced almonds

Poppy Seed Filling

^{3}/$_4$ cup poppy seeds

^{3}/$_4$ cup whole almonds or
    hazelnuts

^{1}/$_2$ cup white sugar

^{1}/$_3$ cup milk

1 teaspoon grated lemon zest

1 tablespoon lemon juice

3 tablespoons unsalted butter

Dissolve the yeast in water with a pinch of sugar. Let stand for 5 minutes, then stir and blend in the milk, salt, sugar, egg, and butter. Gradually beat in about 2^1/$_2$ cups of the flour to make a soft dough.

Turn the dough out onto a lightly floured board and, adding the remaining ^{1}/$_2$ cup flour as necessary, knead until it is smooth and satiny, about 5 minutes. Turn the dough over in a greased bowl, cover, and let it rise in a warm place until doubled (about 1^1/$_2$ hours).

To make the filling: Combine the poppy seeds and almonds or hazelnuts in a blender or food processor and blend until the mixture is the consistency of cornmeal. In a small pan, combine with the rest of the filling ingredients and cook over low heat, stirring until the mixture boils and thickens, about 10 minutes. Cool.

When the dough has risen sufficiently, punch it down. On a flat, greased, sideless 10- by 15-inch pan, roll the dough out to cover the entire surface. Mark the dough lightly into 3 lengthwise sections. Spread the filling over the center third of the dough. Cut about 10 diagonal strips in each of the 2 outer sections of the dough, scoring at an angle from the outside almost as far as the filling. Fold these strips up over the filling, alternately, first one side then the other for a braided effect.

Brush the loaf with egg wash and sprinkle the top with almonds. Let the loaf rise, uncovered, in a warm place until it has almost doubled, about 45 minutes.

Bake at 350°F for 30 minutes. Cool on a rack.

Bill Brown's Five-Flour Brown Bread

Makes 6 loaves

Bill Brown is a Canadian who kidnapped Janet McCulloch, one of Cafe Beaujolais's best waitresses. Well, actually he married her in Canada, moved to the Mendocino area, then took her back to Victoria with him. Our loss; Canada's gain. Bill is an English and math teacher, a poetry fiend, a carpenter, a plumber, an electrician, and—perhaps most important—a creative bread baker.

As I was working on the first edition of this book, he would present me with a loaf of his magical bread every few days, always asking if I were sure I *really* wanted it. He was genuinely concerned that I would spurn any bread that didn't come from our own then-brand-new wood-fired brick oven. Ha! I would delightedly cut a few slices from his hearty loaves, toast them, and dine contentedly with a cup of tea. They nourished me and kept me going for hours at a time. Fortunately, Bill has decided to share his bread with you, too.

2 cups warm water, 110°F

2 tablespoons sugar, honey, or molasses

2 tablespoons dry yeast (check expiration date)

5 cups flour (not white), grain, and/or cereal comprised of 1 cup each of any 5 of these: rye, whole-wheat, soy, seven-grain, bulgur, granola, Grape-Nuts, wheat germ, Cheerios, All-Bran, Shredded Wheat

1 cup sunflower seeds

2 tablespoons salt

2 cups raisins (optional)

4 cups hot water

About 13 cups white flour

In a medium-sized bowl, mix the warm water and sugar. Add the yeast and stir. Set aside in a warm place for 10 minutes.

In a large bowl, place the 5 cups of your chosen ingredients, the sunflower seeds, salt, and the raisins if you are including them. Add the hot water and stir with a wooden spoon until the mixture resembles porridge. Let cool until lukewarm. Stir the yeast mixture and add it to the porridge, mixing thoroughly. Gradually begin adding the white flour, stirring until it becomes impossible to do so any longer.

Turn the sticky dough onto a floured board, scraping out the bowl thoroughly. Knead in as much flour as it takes to make the dough smooth and no longer sticky. You must knead for 5 minutes after the last addition of flour. When ready, the dough will be elastic and springy, with air bubbles visible under the surface—and you will be tired.

Place the dough in a large, lightly greased bowl. Turn the dough to grease its entire surface. Cover with a dry towel and let rise in a warm place until dough has doubled, about 1 hour. Punch it down and let it rise until doubled again, about 45 minutes. Punch it down, turn it out, and knead a few more times.

Divide the dough into 6 equal portions and form each into fat 8-inch-long cigar-shaped pieces. Place in greased 4- by 8-inch bread pans, making sure that the ends of the dough touch the ends of the pan. Cover the pans, and let the loaves rise until the dough has almost doubled, about 45 minutes.

Preheat the oven to 375°F. Bake for 40 minutes on the lower rack, until tops and bottoms are richly browned. (After 40 minutes you can turn them out and check.) Tap the bottoms; they should sound hollow. If not, return to the oven for another 5 minutes and check again. Turn out and cool thoroughly on racks. Freeze whatever you don't plan to use within 2 days.

Don't Worry About Mistakes

I think the real reason that some of us never let ourselves become great cooks is the fear of making mistakes. In the course of becoming a good cook, you are going to make a *lot* of mistakes and ruin, at least mangle, a *lot* of perfectly good ingredients. Some people seem to need permission to goof up. This has always struck me as funny, because no one would expect to learn to paint or draw without wasting some paper, or dance without stepping on a few toes. But in the kitchen, we expect to be perfect from the start and are ashamed when we aren't. The good news is, you may not have to throw out all your mistakes. When those first few crêpes come out of the pan either a little too thin or little too thick, you can freeze them (they're still edible) and use them cut into strips as a garnish for soup. If you overbake the bread, you can turn it into croutons. And there is always the ever-appreciative family dog or cat. In fact, John Bear and his wife, Marina, wrote a book of such hints: *How to Repair Food.*

Corn Bread

Makes one 9-inch pan

Cornmeal used to appear on our menus at the Cafe almost daily, in pancakes, waffles, breads, and entrées. One of the things I love about corn bread is that, while delicious in itself, it also manages to provide an inspirational starting point for other dishes. While testing this recipe, I ran into former Beaujolais employee, Sarah Grimes, on one of my almost daily visits to our local organic grocery store, Corners of the Mouth. Coincidentally, she was making this recipe at home and mentioned her variation, which sounded too tasty not to share with you. Sarah sautés onions, peppers, and sausages (and feel free to add any other vegetables), transfers the mixture to an ovenproof baking dish, covers it with the corn bread batter, then bakes this heavenly preparation until done. Yum!

Gifted cook Jocelyn Kamstra Sugrue, who was the day kitchen manager at the restaurant for many years, would sauté $1/2$ cup of frozen corn in 2 tablespoons of butter and mix it into the batter, intensifying the cornyness. You see, it's as I said, there's something about corn bread that brings out the creativity in people.

3 tablespoons white sugar

$1/2$ cup melted unsalted butter or canola oil

2 large eggs, beaten

1 cup buttermilk

$1^1/3$ cups white flour

$2^1/2$ teaspoons baking powder

$1/2$ teaspoon baking soda

$3/4$ teaspoon salt

$1^1/2$ cups cornmeal

Preheat the oven to 400°F.

Blend together the sugar, butter, eggs, and buttermilk. Sift together the flour, baking powder, baking soda, and salt. Stir in corn meal. Add the dry ingredients to the wet, stir just till blended and the batter is thick, and transfer to a greased 9-inch square pan.

Bake for about 25 to 30 minutes, until top is lightly browned. To avoid dryness, avoid overbaking.

Jocelyn's Orange-Currant Scones

Makes 16 scones

Once we introduced these scones, developed by Jocelyn Kamstra Sugrue, to our brunch customers at the Cafe, they never left the menu.

4 cups white flour

6 tablespoons white sugar

2 tablespoons baking powder

1 teaspoon salt

1 cup cold unsalted butter, cut into teaspoon-sized pieces

4 large eggs

1 cup heavy cream, unwhipped

Grated zest of 3 oranges

1 teaspoon orange extract

$1/2$ cup currants

Egg wash: 1 large egg mixed with 2 tablespoons heavy cream

Extra white sugar for sprinkling on top

Preheat the oven to 425°F.

In a food processor, combine the flour, sugar, baking powder, and salt. Add the cold butter and pulse until the butter is cut in but a dough has not formed. Turn this mixture into a mixing bowl.

In a small bowl, blend together the eggs, cream, zest, orange extract, and currants. Add to the dry ingredients and mix just until a wet dough is formed. You can do this by hand or with a heavy-duty mixer and paddle.

Turn the dough out onto a lightly floured board and knead gently a few times, until the dough becomes workable. Divide the dough in half and refrigerate one of the portions. Roll out the remaining portion to a thickness of about $3/4$ inch, either with a rolling pin or by patting it with your hands.

Cut into 8 wedges. Place the wedges on parchment paper on a 10- by 15-inch pan, brush with the egg wash, and sprinkle lightly with sugar.

Bake for 10 to 15 minutes, until golden brown.

Repeat with the other portion, or freeze it for a later date, wrapping carefully. Defrost in the refrigerator before using.

Polish Raisin Bread

Makes 3 loaves

This is a traditional Polish bread, quite rich, with a light and elegant cakelike crumb, especially when toasted. The recipe comes from my friend, Lorraine Ardaiz, past manager of the Cafe Beaujolais Bakery. My initial suggestion, to add cinnamon, was met with horror. "But that's not Polish!" Lorraine shrieked. Hey, am I an iconoclast or what? Between you and me, I broke with tradition and added lemon zest, and you should too. Just don't tell Lorraine.

2 (2^1/$_4$-teaspoon) packets dry yeast (check expiration date)

^{1}/$_2$ cup warm water, 110°F

1 cup lukewarm milk

2 teaspoons finely grated lemon zest

^{1}/$_2$ cup unsalted butter, softened

2 teaspoons salt

1 cup white sugar

7 large eggs (1 is for the glaze)

About 9 cups white flour

1^3/$_4$ cups raisins

Dissolve the yeast and a pinch of the sugar in a small bowl with the warm water. Set in a warm place for about 5 minutes. It should look active, that is, bubbly. If it isn't, wait another minute or two. Still not bubbly? Discard, and start over.

In a large mixing bowl, whisk together the milk, lemon zest, butter, salt, sugar, and 6 of the eggs. Add the yeast and 3 cups of the flour. Beat for 2 minutes, until very smooth. Replace the whisk with a heavy wooden spoon and gradually beat in about 3^1/$_2$ cups of flour. When the dough is too stiff to beat with the spoon, turn it out onto a lightly floured surface and knead for 10 minutes, adding flour as required.

Place the dough in a large greased bowl. Turn the dough so that all sides are shiny. Cover with a dry towel and set aside in a warm place to rise for about 2 hours, or until just doubled.

Preheat the oven to 350°F.

Punch the dough down and turn it out, kneading a few times to remove air bubbles. Knead in the raisins until evenly distributed.

Divide the dough evenly into 3 portions and shape into loaves. Place each loaf in a greased 8- by 4-inch bread pan. With your finger, poke any fugitive raisins back into the dough to prevent burning. Cover with a towel, and let rise in a warm place until doubled, about 1^1/$_2$ hours.

Beat the remaining egg and gently brush onto the top of each loaf.

Bake for about 35 to 40 minutes, or until the loaves are richly browned on the bottom as well as the top. If the tops brown too quickly, cover loosely with a sheet of foil.

When done, remove pans from oven and place on a cooling rack for 5 minutes. Then remove loaves from pans, turn them on their sides, and let cool fully on a rack.

Read Carefully to Save Yourself Some Grief

From the time I began teaching cooking classes at the First Unitarian Church in Kensington, California, around 1970, I noticed how bewildered people get when it comes to bread dough. Because the dough is too accommodating, it's easy to incorporate far more flour than necessary, resulting in a dry, heavy loaf. The trick is to know when enough's enough.

When I first started to bake bread, my mom came to the rescue, giving me homespun advice that actually has a scientific principle behind it. Once the dough is turned out and kneaded a bit, additional flour is often added. At a certain point, though, you will wonder how much more to add. If the dough is holding together in a ball, and you have kneaded it for about 5 minutes, even if it is still a little sticky, *stop,* cover loosely with a dry towel, and leave it alone for 5 minutes. When you return and knead it just a bit, 99 times out of 100 you will discover dough that is perfect. What my mom "discovered" is *autolysis,* the resting period during which the flour fully absorbs the liquids.

But wait, there's more. As an assurance that you are on the right track, she also recommends that you place your hand on the ball of dough (after it's taken its 5-minute break and been kneaded a bit), and let it rest there for 5 seconds. Remove your hand from the dough, and if it comes off with little or no dough attached to it, the dough is ready.

Cindy's Cherry Chocolate-Chip Scones

Makes 24 scones

Mendocino's bed-and-breakfast inns serve some of the finest morning meals around. I sometimes wrangle an invitation or make a neighborly visit via the back door, pointedly eyeing some delicious baked treat. While munching happily, we exchange town news and business updates. Cindy and Charles Reinhart, the third generation of gracious and hospitable owners of the Joshua Grindle Inn, contributed this often-requested recipe.

1 large egg

1 1/2 cups buttermilk

2 teaspoons almond extract

4 cups white flour

4 teaspoons baking powder

1 teaspoon baking soda

1 teaspoon salt

1/2 cup sugar

1 1/2 cups cold unsalted butter, cut into tablespoon-sized pieces

1 cup semisweet chocolate chips

1 cup chopped dried cherries or dried cranberries

Heavy cream to brush on dough before baking

Sugar to sprinkle on dough before baking

Preheat the oven to 425°F.

Beat together egg, buttermilk, and almond extract.

Combine flour, baking powder, soda, salt, and sugar in a food processor. Cut in the butter until the mixture resembles coarse crumbs.

Turn the flour mixture into a large bowl, add the egg mixture, and stir with a fork a soft dough forms. Add the chocolate chips and cherries and stir to distribute throughout.

Turn the dough onto a lightly floured surface and knead gently 5 to 6 turns. Divide the dough into quarters and pat into 1/2-inch-thick circles. Cut each circle into 6 wedges.

Place scones on baking sheets lined with parchment paper. Brush with cream and sprinkle with a little sugar.

Bake for 13 to 15 minutes, or until lightly browned. Remove from the oven and serve warm.

Basic Brioche Dough

Makes two 8- by 4-inch loaves

This classic French dough is rich with butter and eggs. It can be used to wrap sausage, cheese, or salmon for savory flavors. Or soak it in liqueur syrup, and fill it with pastry cream and raisins for a sweet sensation. Or just enjoy it "plain" with a little jam. As the primary ingredient in French toast and bread pudding, it adds a great flavor and texture. I made this recipe for a series of wildly popular brioche classes I taught at Linda Carucci's Kitchen, a cooking school in Oakland, California.

Sponge

3/4 cup milk, 110°F

1 (2 1/4-teaspoon) packet yeast (check expiration date)

1 cup unbleached white flour

Dough

1 cup unsalted butter, softened

1 tablespoon sugar

1 3/4 teaspoons salt

1 tablespoon finely grated orange or lemon zest (optional)

1 cup eggs (4 to 5), at room temperature

About 3 3/4 cups unbleached white flour

Pour milk into a small bowl, add yeast, and stir. Set in a warm place for 5 minutes, then check that the yeast is working (see page 31). Add flour, stir to combine, cover bowl with plastic wrap, and set aside at room temperature for 30 minutes, until sponge has risen.

Place butter in a large mixing bowl and beat with a heavy wooden spoon, or use a heavy-duty mixer. Beat in the sugar, salt, zest, and the eggs, followed by the flour. Add the sponge, and continue beating vigorously until the dough is smooth and elastic, about 10 minutes. Scrape the sides of the bowl with a rubber spatula to make sure no bits remain unbeaten, then scrape again near the end of the beating time. Cover with plastic wrap and let rise until almost doubled, about 1 1/2 hours.

When the dough has risen, beat it to remove the air. Cover with plastic wrap and refrigerate. Over the next 3 hours, punch the dough down every 30 minutes. When thoroughly cold, turn the dough out onto a very lightly floured board, knead a few times, form into a flat disc, about 2 inches thick, cover completely in plastic wrap, and place in a plastic bag. Return to the refrigerator where it can remain for up to 24 hours.

When you're ready to form the loaves, remove the dough from the refrigerator and divide in half. Return one portion to the refrigerator. Gently knead the dough and form into a loaf shape, 8 inches long. Place in a greased loaf pan. Repeat with the remaining portion of dough. Let rise in a warm place for about 1 1/2 hours, until doubled in bulk.

Preheat the oven to 350°F. Bake loaves for about 35 to 40 minutes, until deep golden brown. Remove from pans and let cool on a wire rack.

Gramma Carroll's Cinnamon Rolls

Makes 12 rolls

When my friend Michael Carroll told me about his grandmother's legendary cinnamon rolls, I knew they had to be in the book. That was even before I learned of her background—years of cooking all day long for hard-working, famished cowboys and ranch hands in Big Sky country. But nothing prepared me for the size of her original recipe, which started with: "Take 17 cups liquid...." The amount of flour needed to turn *that* into dough would require a bathtub to mix it in, not to mention a backhoe to knead it with! This version offers more manageable portions and yields rolls with a tender crumb and just the right amount of cinnamon and sugar. If you prefer more filling, increase the cinnamon and sugar by 50 percent.

1 cup warm water, 110°F

1 (2^1/4-teaspoon) packet dry active
   yeast (check expiration date)

3 tablespoons sugar

1^1/4 cups whole milk

2 tablespoons unsalted butter,
   softened, and cut into
   teaspoon-sized pieces

1^1/2 teaspoons salt

About 5^1/4 cups white flour

Filling

^{3}/4 cup unsalted butter, softened

^{3}/4 cup white sugar mixed with
   3 tablespoons cinnamon

Sprinkle yeast over warm water, add a pinch of the sugar, stir, and let sit in a warm place for 5 minutes, until bubbly.

Meanwhile, over medium heat, scald the milk by heating to just below the boiling point. Bubbles will form around the outside of the milk. Remove from heat and let cool to just warm, about 110°F.

In a large bowl, place sugar, milk, butter, salt, and yeast. With a heavy wooden spoon or a wire whisk, stir to combine, then add 2^1/2 cups of flour. Beat vigorously for about 2 minutes. With the spoon, add more flour gradually, about ^{1}/2 cup at a time. When the dough is too stiff to stir, turn the dough out onto a lightly floured board and begin to knead the dough. Add flour *only as absolutely necessary* to prevent the dough from sticking to the board.

After the last addition of flour, knead for 5 minutes. Place in a greased bowl, turning the dough to grease all sides. Cover tightly with plastic wrap; write the time on the wrap with a marking pen, and set aside in a warm place, 85°F, until doubled in size, about 1^1/2 hours.

Punch down, turn out, and knead a few times to remove air bubbles. Divide dough in half, return one portion to the bowl, and cover. Knead the dough that's on your board, just a few times to form it into a neat ball. With a rolling pin, begin to roll out the dough. The breadboard will need just a bit of flour to prevent sticking, but be stingy to avoid adding too much flour. Roll out the dough to 10 by 16 inches, and about ^{3}/8 inch thick. At first, the dough will be so resilient, it will spring back to its original small size and you will wonder how it can ever reach these dimensions. However, it will relax over the next few minutes and become more manageable.

When the dough is rolled out, spread half the butter for the filling over the surface, all the way to the edges. This is easy to do with a metal or rubber spatula, although I have also used a 4-inch plastic putty knife. Sprinkle half the cinnamon-sugar mixture evenly over the surface to cover the butter. Starting from a wide end, roll up the dough. This may seem awkward; however, about a quarter of the way along, the dough will become firmer and make a neater roll. With each revolution, pause and press the dough to secure the filling. If the filling starts to escape from the ends, just push it back in.

With a sharp knife, cut the roll into 6 pieces. Place each piece, cut-side down, into a 9- by 13-inch pan and cover with a towel.

Repeat procedure with the other portion of dough.

Place each pan in a warm spot and let pieces rise for about 1 hour, until doubled, very puffy, and light.

Preheat the oven to 350°F. Bake for about 30 to 35 minutes until browned.

Of Bread and Chocolate

Cultural culinary differences are often startling, even life altering. For example, the first time (in my teens) I was offered a chunk of chocolate with fresh, crusty bread—a traditional Spanish treat— I was so blown away by the combination, I can still remember exactly where I was sitting and what time of day it was (morning, of course).

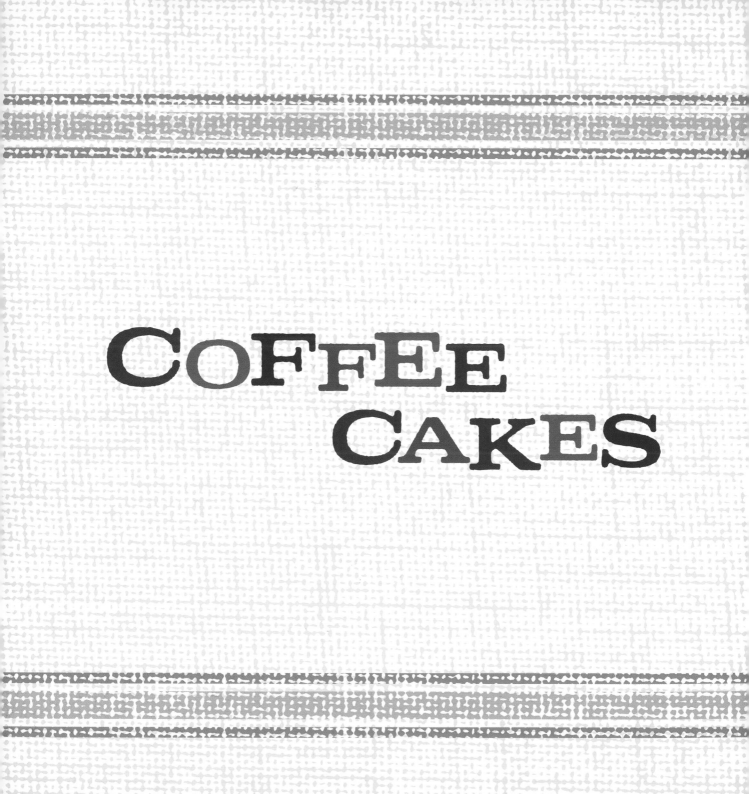

COFFEE CAKES

Chocolate Coffee Cake
50

Blueberry Cream Cheese
Coffee Cake
51

Buttermilk-Cinnamon
Coffee Cake
52

Yogurt Coffee Cake
54

Rachel's Version of the
Anchorage Petroleum Wives'
Club Coffee Cake
55

Streusel-Caramel Coffee Cake
& Caramel Sauce
56

Almond- or Chocolate-filled
Coffee Cake
57

Yeasted Apple-Raisin Cake
58

Chocolate Coffee Cake

Makes 1 cake that serves 12 generously

I like to think of this cake as having everything sweet you've ever wanted in one dish: It has chocolate; it has apricots; it has almonds. What with chocolate chips *and* cocoa, there's no question about how chocolatey it is—it is definitely chocolatey. The chips pretty much melt into the batter, so there aren't discrete chips left after baking, just more chocolate in the cake. It's also very elegant—the sort of thing you could serve at a dignified tea.

I suggest making this cake in a Bundt pan, but a rectangular 9- by 13-inch coffee cake pan is fine, too. It will taste the same, of course; it just won't look as fancy. But since it will probably be around for about nine minutes anyway, what's the difference?

Nut Filling

3/4 cup firmly packed light brown sugar

1 tablespoon cinnamon

2 tablespoons powdered instant coffee

3 tablespoons chopped dried apricots

2 tablespoons unsweetened cocoa

1 cup coarsely chopped toasted almonds

1/4 cup semisweet chocolate chips

Cake Batter

2 3/4 cups white flour

1 1/2 teaspoons baking powder

1 1/2 teaspoons baking soda

1/2 teaspoon salt

3/4 cup unsalted butter, softened

1 1/2 cups white sugar

1 teaspoon vanilla extract

3 large eggs

2 cups plain yogurt

Preheat the oven to 350°F. Mix together all the ingredients for the nut filling and set aside.

Sift together the flour, baking powder, baking soda, and salt, and set aside. In the bowl of an electric mixer, beat the butter until very light and fluffy. Add the sugar and vanilla and beat for 2 minutes. Add the eggs and continue beating for another 2 minutes. This mixture must be very smooth.

Gradually add the flour mixture, alternating with the yogurt, and beat only until the mixture is smooth after each addition.

Generously butter a 10-inch Bundt pan or 9- by 13-inch coffee cake pan, and pour the batter and filling into the pan in the following way: batter, filling, batter, filling, batter.

Bake for about 1 hour and 10 minutes or 40 to 45 minutes for a 9- by 13-inch cake. Use the toothpick test to ensure the cake is completely baked. Cool on a rack for 10 minutes, then turn out with care.

To serve, sift powdered sugar lightly over the top of the cake. Best served warm.

Blueberry Cream Cheese Coffee Cake

Makes 1 cake that serves 10 to 12

This divine cake is from talented baker Elaine Wing Hillesland of Alegria Oceanfront Inn and Cottages, one of Mendocino's most welcoming inns, and a favorite place I just "happen" to drop by for a chat in time to sample a breakfast treat.

1 cup fresh or frozen blueberries*

1/4 cup apple juice

1 teaspoon cornstarch

2 teaspoons water

2 1/4 cups white flour

3/4 cup sugar

1/2 cup cold unsalted butter, cut into 1/2-tablespoon-sized slices

1/2 teaspoon baking powder

1/2 teaspoon baking soda

1/4 teaspoon salt

Zest of 1 lemon

3/4 cup plain low-fat yogurt

1 teaspoon vanilla extract

1 large egg, beaten

6 ounces (by weight) cream cheese, softened

1/4 cup sugar

1 large egg

1/2 teaspoon lemon juice

1/2 cup sliced almonds

---

* You may use raspberries instead, in which case add 1/4 cup sugar and 1 tablespoon orange liqueur

Preheat oven to 350°F.

Grease and flour a 9-inch springform pan.

Place the blueberries and apple juice in a small saucepan over medium heat, and bring to a boil. Reduce the heat and let simmer over very low heat for 3 minutes, stirring occasionally.

Combine the cornstarch and water and add 2 tablespoons of the warm blueberry juice to the mixture, stir, then add the mixture to the blueberries. Stir, and simmer until reduced to 3/4 cup of goop, about 1 minute. Set aside.

Place flour and sugar in a food processor and combine. Add butter and pulse until the mixture resembles coarse crumbs. Reserve 1 cup of this mixture in a small bowl for the topping. Pour the remaining mixture into a large bowl. Retain the bowl for use later; don't bother washing. Stir in the baking powder, baking soda, salt, and lemon zest.

Beat the yogurt, vanilla, and egg together, and stir in. The batter will be thick. Using a small stainless steel offset spatula or a 4-inch plastic putty knife, spread evenly along the bottom of the prepared pan, then up the sides about 1/4 inch, creating a "well."

Whirl the cream cheese, sugar, egg, and lemon juice in the food processor until smooth. Spread over the well of batter to within about 1/4 inch of the sides.

Carefully pour the blueberry goop over the cream cheese mixture. It will be uneven and won't cover the cream cheese completely. Drag the putty knife, or flat edge of the spatula, to move the goop around.

Toss together the sliced almonds with the reserved crumb mixture. Sprinkle over the blueberry topping and exposed batter edge.

Bake for 40 to 45 minutes, or until the filling is set and the cake is a light golden brown. Let cool on a rack for 10 minutes before removing sides.

Buttermilk-Cinnamon Coffee Cake

Makes 1 cake that serves 12

No one can claim to be a former member of the Cafe Beaujolais Fan Club without devouring at least two pieces of this addictive coffee cake. We actually tried to stop making it, but our customers wouldn't let us.

$2^1/4$ cups white flour

$^1/2$ teaspoon salt

2 teaspoons cinnamon

$^1/4$ teaspoon powdered ginger

1 cup firmly packed brown sugar

$^3/4$ cup white sugar

$^3/4$ cup canola oil

1 cup chopped walnuts or pecans

1 teaspoon baking soda

1 teaspoon baking powder

1 large egg, beaten

1 cup buttermilk

In a large bowl, mix together the flour, salt, 1 teaspoon of the cinnamon, ginger, both sugars, and canola oil. Remove $^3/4$ cup of this mixture, and to it add the nuts and the remaining teaspoon of cinnamon. Mix well, and set aside to use as a topping.

To the remaining batter, add the baking soda, baking powder, egg, and buttermilk. Mix to combine all ingredients. Small lumps in the batter are okay.

Pour the batter into a well-greased 9- by 13- by 2-inch pan. Sprinkle the topping mixture evenly over the surface. Bake at 350°F for 40 to 45 minutes.

Yogurt Coffee Cake

Makes 1 cake that serves 12

This recipe has been in my files so long that I honestly can't remember where it came from. The original called for sour cream, but I found I can substitute low-fat yogurt without any detectable change whatsoever.

$1^1/_4$ cups plain yogurt

$1^1/_4$ teaspoons baking soda, sifted

$1/_2$ cup butter, softened

$1^1/_4$ cups white sugar

$1/_2$ teaspoon salt

2 large eggs, beaten

$1^3/_4$ cups white flour

$1^3/_4$ teaspoons baking powder

$2/_3$ cup semisweet chocolate chips
   (optional)

Topping

$1/_2$ cup chopped nuts

1 teaspoon cinnamon

$1/_3$ cup firmly packed light brown
   sugar

Preheat the oven to 350°F.

In a large bowl, mix together the yogurt and baking soda, and set aside.

Cream together the butter, sugar, salt, and eggs until fluffy. In a separate bowl, sift together the flour and baking powder, add to the butter mixture, and blend. Quickly stir in the yogurt and soda.

Pour into a greased 9- by 13-inch pan. If you are using chocolate chips, sprinkle evenly over the surface and press them lightly into batter. Combine the topping ingredients and sprinkle it evenly on the surface. Bake about 40 to 45 minutes, until it tests done with a toothpick.

Rachel's Version of the Anchorage Petroleum Wives' Club Coffee Cake

Makes 2 cakes, each serves 12

The talented Rachel Binah first encountered this cake while visiting her sister in Alaska. It appealed to her sense of irony because she was at that time a leader in the Ocean Sanctuary movement.

This yeasted cake has a choice of two fillings and an attractive presentation that results from folding the dough strips into a lattice pattern. You can freeze the cakes when assembled but not yet risen. Defrost at room temperature overnight, then bake in the morning.

2 (2^1/4-teaspoon) packets yeast (check expiration date)

^{1}/2 cup warm water, 110°F

^{1}/4 cup sugar

5 cups white flour

1 teaspoon salt

1 cup unsalted butter

8 ounces (by weight) cream cheese

1 large egg

1 teaspoon vanilla extract

1 cup buttermilk

Apricot-Almond or Prune-Pecan Filling

2^1/4 cups dried, pitted apricots or prunes

^{3}/4 cup sugar

1^1/2 cups orange juice

1^1/2 cups chopped nuts

Icing

^{1}/2 cup powdered sugar, mixed with 1 tablespoon lemon juice

In a small bowl, sprinkle the yeast over the warm water, add a pinch of the sugar, and stir. Set aside for 5 minutes until foamy.

In a large bowl, stir together the flour, the rest of the sugar, and salt. Using a hand mixer, cut in the butter and cream cheese. You can also place the dry ingredients in a food processor and cut in the butter and cream cheese.

Combine yeast, egg, vanilla, and buttermilk and add to flour mixture, stirring to combine. Knead for 5 minutes on a lightly floured surface. Place the dough in a greased bowl and turn to grease the top. Cover the bowl with a dry towel and let it rise for about 1^1/4 hours, or until doubled.

To prepare the filling: Chop the fruit and mix with the sugar. Place in a small pot with the juice and cook until the juice has almost evaporated, stirring occasionally. Add the nuts, and set aside to cool.

Punch the dough down and divide it into 2 portions. Using 2 large greased cookie sheets, roll out each portion directly onto a cookie sheet into a rectangle that measures about 12 by 15 by ^{1}/4 inch. Spread the filling evenly along the middle third of the dough.

Along each side of the filling, cut the dough into about 20 strips at an angle from the outside to just where the filling begins. Fold a strip from the left side over the center filling, then one from the right side, and so on, making a lattice pattern of the strips.

Cover each coffee cake with a towel. Let them rise until doubled, about 1 hour. Preheat the oven to 350°F. Bake for about 55 to 60 minutes, or until golden brown.

Remove from oven, let cool for 10 minutes, then drizzle with the icing.

Streusel-Caramel Coffee Cake & Caramel Sauce

Makes one 8-inch pan that serves 9 to 12

The best gauge of recipe-testing success is the speed with which the finished product disappears. This coffee cake clocked in at about seven minutes.

The recipe is unusual in that the caramel sauce is actually in the batter, rather than the topping. The sauce disappears from sight, but the taste is quite wonderful.

My friend Barbara Holzrichter used to have a tiny little business that made the world's best butter cream caramels. Alas, this is no more. This recipe was originally made with her caramels. The present version is made with a delicious caramel sauce.

Cake Batter

3/4 cup white sugar

1/4 cup unsalted butter, softened

1 large egg

1/2 cup milk

1 1/2 cups white flour

2 teaspoons baking powder

1/2 teaspoon salt

1/2 cup warm Caramel Sauce (below)

Streusel Mixture

1 cup brown sugar

1/4 cup white flour

2 teaspoons cinnamon

1/2 cup melted unsalted butter

1 cup chopped walnuts

Preheat oven to 350°F.

Butter an 8-inch square pan.

With an electric mixer, beat together the sugar, butter, and egg; add the milk. Sift together the flour, baking powder, and salt, then blend into the butter mixture.

Spread two-thirds of the batter in the pan. Pour the caramel sauce evenly over the surface. Mix together the streusel ingredients and, with your hands, evenly distribute it over the surface of the batter. Cover with the remaining batter.

Bake for about 40 to 45 minutes, or until a toothpick in the center comes out clean.

Caramel Sauce   Makes about 1 quart

1 cup light corn syrup

1 1/2 cups white sugar

1/2 teaspoon salt

1/2 cup unsalted butter

2 cups heavy cream, divided in half

1 teaspoon vanilla

In a saucepan over low heat, stir together corn syrup, sugar, salt, butter, and 1 cup of the heavy cream. Cook until the mixture reaches the soft ball stage, 234°F, about 20 minutes.

Stir in the remaining cup of heavy cream and cook to a thick, smooth consistency, 228 to 230°F, about 20 minutes.

Remove from heat, and stir in the vanilla.

Almond- or Chocolate-filled Coffee Cake

Makes 1 cake that serves 8

Another variation on the theme...and another opportunity to start the day with some chocolate.

8 ounces blanched almonds

1/2 cup sugar

1 teaspoon lemon juice

1 teaspoon almond extract

1/3 cup unsalted butter, softened

2 teaspoons white flour

1 teaspoon grated lemon zest, packed

3 tablespoons dry crumbs: fine dry bread, butter cookie, or graham cracker

1 large egg

2 ounces semisweet chocolate chips (optional)

Half of Basic Sweet Roll Dough (page 30) made with lemon, instead of orange, zest

1 tablespoon melted unsalted butter

Glaze: 1 beaten egg with 1 table-spoon milk

Preheat the oven to 350°F. Place the almonds and sugar in a food processor and process until the mixture resembles course meal. Add the lemon juice, almond extract, softened butter, flour, lemon zest, crumbs, egg, and chocolate chips. Process until the mixture is combined. If you are using chocolate, little lumps may remain. Set aside.

On a lightly floured board, roll the dough into a 10- by 16-inch rectangle. The dough will be elastic and difficult to roll out. If it fights you every inch of the way, cover with a dry towel and let it rest for about 5 minutes, after which time you should have no problem rolling the dough to the proper size.

Brush with melted butter, and spread the filling evenly over the surface, except for a 1-inch-wide strip along one of the 10-inch sides. Starting with the other 10-inch side, roll the dough toward you as tightly as is reasonable, taking care not to squish the filling out of the roll. Pinch the seam and place the roll, seam-side down, on a greased 10- by 15-inch baking sheet.

While the roll is lying flat on the sheet, bend it around into a circle, like a giant doughnut, and pinch the ends together. Hold a knife vertically and cut from the outside to the inside, about three-fourths of the way through the circle, making 11 incisions (see illustration below).

Step 1	Step 2	Step 3

Cover with a dry towel and let the loaf rise in a warm place for about 1 hour, until puffy and about doubled in size. Brush gently with the glaze, taking care not to let it run onto the pan. Bake for 25 to 30 minutes, or until richly browned. Remove from the oven. Leave the coffee cake on the pan and set on a rack to cool.

Yeasted Apple-Raisin Cake

Makes 1 cake that serves 10 to 12

An antique apple orchard lies in the meadow on the east side of my house in Mendocino. Every September, as the 2,000 pounds (no exaggeration!) of fruit ripened, the question arose at the restaurant, "What the heck are we going to do with all this?" Breakfast, lunch, and dinner suddenly became apple-intensive meals. Apple butter, chutney, crisps, sauce, sautéed slices, muffins, and coffee cakes—sometimes the bounty seemed like a burden. But we did use up a huge portion of the apples, and turned the remainder into juice at the end of the season.

Dough

1 (2^1/$_4$-teaspoon) packet dry yeast
   (check expiration date)

1 teaspoon white sugar

^{1}/$_3$ cup warm water, 110°F

^{1}/$_3$ cup warm milk, 110°F

3 large eggs, at room temperature

1^3/$_4$ cups white flour

^{3}/$_4$ teaspoon salt

^{1}/$_3$ cup unsalted butter, softened

Filling

3 pounds tart apples (about 8),
   peeled, cored, and quartered

2 tablespoons lemon juice

^{1}/$_4$ cup brandy

^{1}/$_2$ cup apple juice

2^1/$_2$ cups white sugar

^{1}/$_2$ cup water

^{1}/$_2$ cup raisins

Topping

About 1^1/$_2$ cups whipping cream
   mixed with 2^1/$_2$ teaspoons
   vanilla, or Crème Fraîche
   (page 135)

Freshly grated nutmeg

In a small bowl, dissolve the yeast and sugar in the warm water, stir, and set aside for a few minutes, until foamy.

In a large bowl, place the milk, eggs, flour, and salt. Whisk until blended, add the softened and foamy yeast and butter, and whisk for 4 minutes. The batter should be perfectly smooth and strands of elastic dough should be visibly pulling around the outside of the bowl. With a rubber spatula, scrape down the sides of the bowl. Cover the bowl tightly with plastic wrap. Let the batter rise in a warm place until doubled, about 1^1/$_4$ hours.

After covering the bowl of rising dough tightly with plastic wrap, I write the time on the wrap with a marker. That way I always remember how long something has been rising. This may be more of an issue in a busy commercial kitchen, but I do it at home, too.

While the dough is rising, prepare the apples, mix the lemon juice, brandy, and apple juice, and set aside.

In a heavy-bottomed pan over low heat, mix together the sugar and water until the sugar dissolves.

Bring to a boil and continue cooking, without stirring, over medium heat, using a brush dipped in water to wash down the crystals that have formed on the side of the pan.

When the sugar and water mixture is a rich caramel color, turn off the heat and *carefully* add the apples, then the lemon juice and brandy mixture, taking great care to avoid splattering the incredibly hot sugar syrup. Stir to coat the apples, as best you can. The syrup "seizes up" and it looks like an awful mess, but don't despair. Cover, and cook at medium heat for 10 minutes to soften the apples slightly

and dissolve the hardened sugar. Stir carefully a few times during this process. Add the raisins.

Pour the apple compote into a lightly buttered 9- by 13-inch pan. Let the mixture cool to room temperature, about 45 minutes. Turn the apples cut-side up, so that the attractive, rounded side will show when you turn them out after baking. To speed up the process, place in the refrigerator.

When the dough has doubled, beat it down with a wooden spoon and pour it over the room-temperature compote.

Preheat the oven to 350°F.

Let the cake rise in a warm place until the dough is puffy, about 45 minutes. Don't cover with plastic wrap because if the batter touches it, it will stick and make a mess.

Gently place the pan in the oven and bake for about 35 minutes, until golden brown.

Remove from the oven and let cool on a wire rack for 20 minutes. With great care, and no children or animals of any size nearby, invert the cake quickly onto a large flat pan or plate. Serve warm with the whipping cream or crème fraîche, topped with nutmeg. I don't add any sweetening to either creams because the cake is very sweet.

PANCAKES, WAFFLES, FRENCH TOAST & CRÊPES

Cottage Cheese Pancakes
62

Oma Leah's Potato Pancakes
63

Pumpkin & Ginger Pancakes
64

Very Berry Pancakes
65

Heidi's Baked Sunday Pancake
66

Light-as-a-Feather Whole-Wheat
& Wild Rice Waffles
67

Tropical Waffles
with Macadamia Nuts
& Toasted Coconut
68

Banana-Pecan Pineapple Ice
Cream Waffle Sundae
69

French Toasts
72

Dutch Apple & Bacon Pancakes
75

Egg Pancakes à la Hilde & David
76

Trou Pain Perdu
77

Buckwheat Crêpes with
Spinach-Dill Scramble
78

Cottage Cheese Pancakes

Makes about 10 pancakes

In my late teens, I lived for two years with a wonderful Berkeley family, the Nelsons, as an *au pair* helper. Mrs. Nelson kept pancake batter on hand in the refrigerator at all times. She made pancakes for her three children *even on school days!* This seemed incredible to me, as "pancake days" in my family were a very big deal, reserved mostly for special occasions because the pancake griddle was stored far back in a cupboard, making retrieval awkward and infrequent. This recipe is my tribute, and re-creation, of those fabulous pancake days of yesteryear with the Nelson family.

3 large eggs

1 cup cottage cheese (nonfat is fine)

2 tablespoons canola oil (can be omitted)

1/4 cup white flour

1/4 teaspoon baking powder

1/4 teaspoon salt

2 tablespoons ground flax seeds (optional)

Place all the ingredients in a blender or food processor and combine until smooth. Pour the batter onto a lightly greased hot griddle in 3-inch circles. Flip when bottoms are golden brown. Uncharacteristically, bubbles rarely show on the surface when they are ready to be flipped. Plan to peek underneath when you think they should be done.

Batter will keep up to three days refrigerated.

Oma Leah's Potato Pancakes

Makes about 9 pancakes

Oma Leah was my friend Hilde Burton's grandmother, and Hilde passed this recipe along to me when she learned I was looking for a really great potato pancake. Because the best part of a potato pancake is the crispy crunchy part, the trick here is to make each pancake so thin that virtually the entire pancake is crispy and crunchy. These potato pancakes are so good they find their way onto my table not only at breakfast, but at other meals as a side dish when a starch is needed. I especially like them with an entrée that has lots of sauce, such as a chicken stew.

2 large russet potatoes

2 tablespoons grated yellow onions

1 teaspoon white flour

$^1/_4$ teaspoon powdered ginger

$^1/_4$ teaspoon salt

$^1/_4$ teaspoon black pepper

About $^1/_3$ cup canola oil

Peel, then coarsely grate the potatoes to make elongated, very thin strips. Mix with the grated onion. Combine the rest of the ingredients, except oil, and add to the potatoes.

Heat some of the oil in a heavy-bottomed skillet (mine is cast iron and 12 inches across) and, when very hot but not smoking, drop three blobs of mixture into the pan and flatten them out. The pancakes should be about 4 inches in diameter—and thin. If they are too thick, they won't get crisp enough.

Reduce the heat and cook for about 3 minutes. Check that the underside is richly browned before flipping, then cook another 3 minutes on the other side. Continue with the rest of the potato mixture, adding more oil as needed.

Serve with sour cream and applesauce.

Pumpkin & Ginger Pancakes

Makes 12 to 15 pancakes, depending on size

I find myself longing for pumpkin more often than merely once a year at Thanksgiving, when I blissfully demolish my mom's Fabulous Pumpkin Pie (page 184). For years, our remarkably tasty pumpkin muffins had to satisfy my craving because pumpkin pleasure seemed bound by tradition to only one holiday, during one season, plus the occasional quick bread. But that was before I tasted these pumpkin pancakes whipped up by Anne Wertheim Rosenfeld—it was love at first bite. Anne is not only a talented photographer and writer; she knows what to do with pumpkin all year long.

Although I cook with very few processed ingredients, canned pumpkin is one I use without qualms.

1 cup white flour
1/4 teaspoon salt
2 tablespoons dark brown sugar
1 teaspoon baking powder
1/2 teaspoon baking soda
1/2 teaspoon cinnamon
1/4 teaspoon freshly grated nutmeg
1/2 teaspoon powdered ginger
1 large egg, beaten
1/4 cup plain nonfat yogurt
3/4 cup milk
3/4 cup canned pumpkin
2 tablespoons melted butter

In a medium-sized bowl, sift together the flour, salt, sugar, baking powder, baking soda, and spices. In a separate bowl, combine the remaining ingredients. Add the flour mixture, and stir to combine.

Heat the griddle or nonstick pan, then grease. It will be ready to grease when a drop of water flicked on it "skates" across the surface. Use 1 heaping tablespoon of batter to make one silver-dollar-sized pancake. Okay, they're larger than real silver dollars, but that's inflation for you.

Cook over medium heat and flip once bubbles form on the surface. The smaller you make them, the easier they are to flip. Peek underneath because bubbles *don't* appear in this thick batter as rapidly as they do in a thinner one.

Serve with Gingered Butter and warm maple syrup.

Gingered Butter

2 tablespoons finely chopped candied ginger
1/4 cup unsalted butter, softened

Combine the ginger and butter with a wooden spoon, or in a food processor.

Very Berry Pancakes

Makes about 18 pancakes

This recipe can be made with just blueberries, or you can add cranberries for a red, white, and blue (well, red, pancake, and blue) 4th of July breakfast. I wouldn't use the cranberries alone as they're a little too tart.

When berries are added to a batter, they "bleed" color and the batter will take on a distinctly unappetizing grayish cast. For this reason, I freeze the berries before adding them.

How long do frozen berries last? Well, in my parents' freezer, I found a package of berries that had been frozen eight *years* earlier. I used them in these pancakes, and they worked perfectly. Incidentally, my dad is in seventh heaven whenever I test pancake recipes—morning, noon, and night.

$1^1/_2$ cups white flour

$1^1/_2$ tablespoons sugar

$^1/_2$ teaspoon salt

$1^1/_2$ teaspoons baking powder

1 teaspoon baking soda

2 large eggs, separated

2 cups buttermilk

$^1/_4$ cup unsalted butter, melted and cooled

2 cups frozen berries (if cranberries are used, chop them coarsely before adding)

Sift the dry ingredients into a bowl.

In a separate bowl, mix together the egg yolks, buttermilk, and butter. Add the flour mixture to the eggs and blend.

Beat the egg whites until stiff, but not dry, and fold into the batter.

Make pancakes on a properly heated griddle (water sprinkled on it will "skate" around in little beads when the temperature is right).

Sprinkle berries on top, flip when bottoms are golden, and cook until golden brown. Serve on heated plates with warm syrup.

Heidi's Baked Sunday Pancake

Makes 1 pancake that serves 3 to 4

For many years, my friend Heidi and her family lived on a piece of property immediately north of Cafe Beaujolais. Two large sheep grazed in their meadow nearest the restaurant. They bleated regularly, and the sound carried with remarkable clarity directly into my upstairs office. It occurred to me on more than one occasion that this was not an experience shared by many restaurant owners.

These days, Heidi Dickerson is a food, wine, and travel journalist with many books to her credit, among them *Mendocino: The Ultimate Wine and Food Lover's Guide* and *Sonoma: The Ultimate Winery Guide*.

Baked pancakes are the easiest thing in the world to make and yet impressive. I often serve them on Christmas morning because the preparation time is short and the results delicious.

3 tablespoons melted unsalted butter

3 large eggs

3/4 cup milk

1 1/2 tablespoons sugar

1/2 cup white flour

1/2 teaspoon vanilla extract

Pinch of salt

Preheat the oven to 475°F.

Brush butter on the bottom and sides of a 10-inch cast-iron frying pan with an ovenproof handle.

In a mixing bowl, beat the eggs until light and lemon-colored. Add the remaining ingredients and beat until smooth.

Pour the batter into the pan.

Bake at 475°F for 5 minutes, then lower the temperature to 400°F. Bake for 10 minutes, then lower the temperature again, to 350°F, and bake for 10 minutes more. The pancake will be puffed and browned.

Run a spatula around the pancake and slide it out onto a serving platter. Sprinkle with powdered sugar and serve at once.

Light-as-a-Feather Whole-Wheat & Wild Rice Waffles

Makes about 7 cups of batter

Whole-wheat flour has developed a reputation for producing foods that are heavy, but this need not be the case. These waffles, for example, are light because the eggs are separated and the whites folded in.

If you have ever tried commercial frozen waffles, I'm sure you'll agree with me that they are, by and large, just awful. And there is no reason to use those horrors when you can keep a large store of homemade waffles in the freezer. Simply make these waffles ahead of time, cool, wrap them in foil, and freeze. When you're ready to serve, place them, unwrapped, directly on the rack of a preheated 350°F oven, and they'll be ready almost at once—within a minute or so.

If you don't have or don't want to use wild rice, you can use toasted nuts or even tame brown rice, although it doesn't have the nice nutty flavor of the wild. (One of our most popular breakfast entrées at the restaurant was a Wild and Crazy Waffle prepared with a sprinkling of both wild rice and toasted pecans.) This recipe can also be used for pancakes.

2 cups whole-wheat flour

2¹/₂ teaspoons baking powder

³/₄ teaspoon baking soda

¹/₂ teaspoon salt

2 tablespoons honey

4 large eggs, separated

1 cup plain yogurt

1¹/₃ cups milk

¹/₃ cup melted unsalted butter, or canola oil, or a combination of the two

1¹/₂ cups cooked wild rice

In a medium-sized bowl, sift together the dry ingredients.

In a separate bowl, blend together the honey, egg yolks, yogurt, milk, and butter. Add the dry mixture to the wet, blending thoroughly. Beat the egg whites until stiff, but not dry. Fold the egg whites into the batter.

Make waffles according to the directions on your waffle maker, sprinkling about 3 tablespoons wild rice per waffle over the batter after it has been poured onto the iron.

Tropical Waffles with Macadamia Nuts & Toasted Coconut

Makes about 8 cups of batter

Cafe Beaujolais customers always seemed to enjoy the different ways we experimented with waffles. Macadamia nuts, expensive and luxurious, happened to be in great supply one year and inspired this recipe. Coconut was also popular, no matter how we served it. Although I don't think of myself as a big fan of coconut, when I do use it I'm surprised all over again by how much I like it. This recipe can also be used for pancakes.

2 cups white flour

2¹/2 teaspoons baking powder

³/4 teaspoon baking soda

¹/2 teaspoon salt

2 tablespoons sugar

4 large eggs, separated

1 cup plain yogurt

1¹/2 cups milk

³/4 cup melted unsalted butter, or canola oil, or a combination of the two

³/4 cup chopped toasted macadamia nuts

¹/2 cup toasted sweetened flaked coconut

Toppings: any combination of mango, papaya, pineapple, or banana cut into chunks

In a medium-sized bowl, sift together the dry ingredients.

In a separate bowl, beat together the egg yolks, yogurt, milk, and butter.

Beat the egg whites until stiff, but not dry.

Add the dry ingredients to the wet, and stir to combine. Fold in the egg whites, along with the nuts and coconut.

Make waffles according to the directions on your waffle maker.

Banana-Pecan Pineapple Ice Cream Waffle Sundae

Makes about 8 cups of batter

A number of years ago, *Food and Wine* magazine interviewed me and requested a new recipe. One morning, I was lying in bed wondering what I was going to concoct, when this recipe floated into my mind. What inspired me? Was it sheer creativity? Or early morning hunger?

If you don't usually eat ice cream for breakfast, the suggestion may shock you. But remember, we all eat sweet things and cold things and creamy things for breakfast, at least once in a while. So what's wrong with a sweet cold dish of ice cream, especially in a luscious creation like this? I complete it with a sauce using fresh pineapple, but you could also use the canned variety that comes in its own juice. This recipe can also be used for pancakes.

2 cups white flour

1 teaspoon cinnamon

1/4 teaspoon nutmeg

2 1/2 teaspoons baking powder

3/4 teaspoon baking soda

1/2 teaspoon salt

1 1/2 tablespoons sugar

4 large eggs, separated

1 cup sour cream

1 1/2 cups milk

1/2 cup unsalted butter, or canola oil, or a combination of the two

1 1/2 cups mashed ripe bananas

1 1/2 cups chopped toasted pecans

To make the waffles: Sift together the flour, cinnamon, nutmeg, baking powder, baking soda, salt, and sugar. Set aside.

In a separate bowl, beat together the egg yolks, sour cream, milk, butter and/or oil, and bananas. Add the pecans, and stir mixture in with the dry ingredients until well blended.

Beat the egg whites until stiff, but not dry, and fold them into the banana mixture. Bake according to the waffle iron manufacturer's directions.

Serve the waffle on a warmed plate with a scoop of vanilla ice cream topped with the Chunky Pineapple Sauce (page 70).

CONTINUED

Banana-Pecan Pineapple Ice Cream Waffle Sundae

Chunky Pineapple Sauce

3¹/2 cups pineapple chunks

³/4 cup Simple Syrup (below)

2 tablespoons plus 1 teaspoon
   lemon juice (more or less,
   depending on the sweetness of
   the pineapple)

1¹/4 cups hand-chopped pineapple

Place the pineapple chunks in a food processor and purée.

Mix together the purée, half a cup of the Simple Syrup, and 2 tablespoons of the lemon juice. Taste to determine if more syrup and/or lemon juice are needed. Stir in the hand-chopped pineapple and warm gently.

Simple Syrup

3 cups sugar

1¹/2 cups water

In a small saucepan over medium heat, stir together the sugar and water until the sugar is dissolved. Turn the heat to high and bring to a boil. Boil, uncovered, and *without stirring* for 5 minutes. Let cool. The syrup will keep for a very long time in the refrigerator.

Industrial-grade Maple Syrup

For being such an integral part of the all-American breakfast, real maple syrup is a rather expensive ingredient. (I guess that's why the fake goo was invented.) In the realm of real, I recommend Grade B maple syrup rather than the more expensive Grade A. Grade B, with its darker color and stronger flavor, packs a maple punch ("industrial grade," my sister calls it). Be sure to warm it before gilding your waffles or pancakes.

French Toasts

Makes 6 servings

Fabulous cook and fellow dog lover Naomi Schwartz used to own The Food Company in Gualala, down the coast from Mendocino. Her toasts are offered in both a savory version, stuffed with goat or cream cheese, and a sweet version, using ricotta and apples. Both versions are quite rich; serve with a green or fruit salad. It takes some care to stuff the bread pocket properly, so don't rush!

Stuffing, either Savory (below) or Sweet (opposite)

1 loaf (1 pound) bread, unsliced, preferably homemade, one or two days old

6 large eggs

1 1/4 cups milk

1/2 teaspoon nutmeg

1/8 teaspoon salt

1 teaspoon vanilla extract (for Sweet Version only)

2 tablespoons unsalted butter

Prepare the stuffing mixture first.

Preheat the oven to 375°F. Slice the bread at an angle, making each slice almost 2 inches thick. Cut each slice in half diagonally. With a small sharp knife, cut a pocket into each half, leaving the crusts intact.

Stuff each triangle with about 2 tablespoons of stuffing mixture or as much as can be inserted without tearing the bread.

Beat together the eggs, milk, nutmeg, salt, and vanilla (if used). Immerse the triangles in the liquid for about 5 minutes. It takes quite a long time for the liquid to soak into the bread thoroughly.

In a large skillet, melt the butter and when hot, add as many slices as will easily fit.

Sauté on both sides until richly browned, then place in the oven for 5 minutes. Garnish with hot mushrooms or apples, and serve.

Stuffing: Savory Version

1 pound goat or cream cheese, or a combination of the two

3 tablespoons minced chives

2 teaspoons fresh minced thyme

2 teaspoons fresh minced dill

Salt

Freshly ground black pepper

2 pounds mushrooms, sliced

3 tablespoons unsalted butter

Mix together all the ingredients except the mushrooms and butter.

Sauté mushrooms in butter until cooked through but not reduced. Add salt and pepper to taste and set aside for garnish.

Stuffing: Sweet Version

1 pound ricotta cheese

1 1/2 teaspoons grated orange zest

1 teaspoon vanilla extract

1 teaspoon almond extract

1/8 teaspoon grated nutmeg

4 medium apples, peeled, cored,
    and thinly sliced

3 tablespoons unsalted butter

1/2 teaspoon cinnamon

2 tablespoons brown sugar

Mix together the cheese, orange zest, vanilla and almond extracts, and nutmeg.

Sauté the apples in butter until softened and cooked all the way through, but not mushy. Add the cinnamon and sugar and cook over low heat for another minute or two, until sugar coats the apple slices evenly. Set aside for garnish.

Maple Culpa, Maple Culpa

When we were little, my sister Emily and I often went with our dad to the International House of Pancakes for weekend breakfasts, while our mom stole a bit of quiet time at home. My dad and I always ordered the more traditional pancake and syrup variations—buttermilk and boysenberry, or buckwheat and maple. But Emily invariably went for the buttermilk with—chocolate chips. I cannot express how this offended me. Even to my young mind, something about this combination didn't work for me. I don't know why it didn't—but it didn't. And I've joked about it a lot over the years, as if I did it right and she did it, well, wrong. As it turns out, Emily was onto something all those decades ago. While fine-tuning the Egg Pancakes à la Hilde & David (page 76), I spied a bag of chocolate chips and sprinkled some on the pancake still in the pan, waited a few seconds, rolled it up, and, in a word—nirvana. Em, I owe you.

Dutch Apple & Bacon Pancakes

Makes 4 pancakes

Charming Amsterdam, where my good friend Kathryn Wentzel has lived and worked for over twenty years, boasts an array of fabulous cuisines. For me, no visit is complete without a meal of *pannekoeken*, the traditional homey Dutch pancake that is filled with everything from berries and whipped cream to Nutella. On my first visit to the Netherlands, Kathryn and her friend Jos drove my daughter and me around the countryside. We stopped in a provincial sixteenth-century village and ate in a cozy "pannekoek house," requisite windmill nearby, where we were greeted by a woman in traditional costume and warmed by a welcoming fire in the hearth. We ordered from a long list of pancakes. Back in the city, when Kathryn prepared this recipe for us, we ate gazing out of our apartment's huge windows overlooking the Prinsengracht canal while boats of all sizes and shapes cruised by on the water below.

1 cup whole milk

1 cup water

1 1/2 cups white flour, or 1 1/4 cups white flour and 1/4 cup whole-wheat flour

1/2 teaspoon salt

1 teaspoon baking powder

2 large eggs, beaten

6 to 9 slices bacon, chopped into 1/2-inch pieces

3 apples, peeled, cored, and thinly sliced

In a small saucepan, combine the milk and water and heat until warm. Pour into a blender.

In a bowl, combine the flour, salt, and baking powder, and add to the wet ingredients along with the eggs. Blend at medium speed until the batter is smooth and lump-free. It should be thinner than pancake batter but thicker than crêpe batter.

Cook the bacon in a 10-inch nonstick pan over medium heat. When crispy, remove the bacon with a slotted spoon and add the apple slices. Sauté until the apples soften and caramelize.

Remove the cooked apples and fat from the pan and combine with the bacon (fat too). Return a quarter of the apple-bacon-fat mixture to the pan and turn up the heat. When the pan is quite hot, pour in 2/3 cup of batter and swirl the pan to coat the contents and the pan bottom. The batter should sizzle when it hits the pan to produce a crispiness around the edges.

Reduce the heat a bit. You will need to regulate it carefully during the cooking. Cook for about 2 minutes until golden brown. Flip, and cook for about 2 minutes more.

Slide out onto a warm plate, sprinkle with powdered sugar and maple syrup, as desired, and enjoy. Repeat for the next 3 pancakes.

Egg Pancakes à la Hilde & David

Makes 9 to 12 pancakes, depending on technique

These heavenly pancakes have been a staple in the Burton household ever since I started showing up there, thirty-five years ago. Hilde and David Burton, whose recipes have appeared in my previous books, have always appreciated fine food and gracious entertaining. Their home is one of my daughter's and my favorite places in the world to hang out. And although David's Remarkable Plum Jam recipe wasn't able to be tested in time for this book's publication, it is available on my web site, www.margaretfox.com.

3 large eggs

3 tablespoons canola oil, plus 1 tablespoon for oiling pan

1/4 teaspoon salt

3/4 cup milk

1 1/2 teaspoons sugar

1 cup white flour

1/2 teaspoon finely grated lemon zest, preferably Meyer lemon

Fillings

Warmed and sweetened fresh berries or other fresh fruit

Jam, honey, syrup

Semisweet chocolate chips (I like Guittard)

Crème Fraîche (page 135)

David's Remarkable Plum Jam

Whisk together all the ingredients, except for the lemon zest, until batter is smooth. Pour through a fine mesh sieve to remove lumps and stir again to combine. Add the zest.

Warm an 8-inch nonstick pan on medium-high heat. Grease the warmed pan very lightly with an oiled paper towel. Pour in a scant 3 tablespoons of batter and quickly swirl around the pan to cover the bottom completely. Turn when pancake begins to brown and cook lightly on the other side. Watch out—overcooking toughens this delicate cake. Slide onto a warmed serving plate when done and roll up with the filling of your choice. When I made my chocolate version, I sprinkled a few chips onto the surface of the pancake after I had flipped it, so they had a few seconds to start melting.

This recipe requires one person to stand at the stove, turning these out. Don't try to keep them hot, just eat as they come out of the pan.

Variation: Separate the eggs. As above, whisk together all the ingredients except for the zest and egg whites. Add the zest to the batter. Beat the egg whites separately to soft peaks and fold into the batter.

Cook as above. Stir gently each time before pouring the batter into the pan so the whites remain incorporated. This technique makes 9 because the thicker batter doesn't go as far.

Trou Pain Perdu

Serves 3 to 4

Robert Reynolds, talented longtime culinary professional who now divides his teaching time between Oregon and France, offers a recipe for French toast that he first tasted in a little house on the shore of Lake Memphremagog in Vermont, prepared with local milk and butter, and garden-fresh fruit. Happily, he has made enough changes that I feel no obligation to call it Memphremagog Toast, although you may do so if you feel a particular affinity for the Memphremagog region. (Note: This may be the only recipe in history to mention Memphremagog three, no, four, times.)

1 baguette, sliced into 1-inch slices

1¹/₂ cups milk

4 large eggs

¹/₄ cup orange juice

¹/₄ cup sugar

Pinch of salt

1 tablespoon vanilla extract

2 tablespoons Grand Marnier (optional)

About 3 tablespoons unsalted butter for sautéing

Place the slices of baguette in a 9- by 13-inch pan.

Whisk together all the other ingredients, except butter, until blended, and pour over the bread. Turn the slices to coat them thoroughly. Cover pan with plastic wrap and refrigerate for at least 1 hour.

Heat 2 tablespoons butter in a large sauté pan. After the butter foams, but before it browns, add the bread. Cook over medium heat and turn slices when golden brown. Add more butter as necessary. Serve when the other side is golden brown. At this point, the bread has a custardy texture, so if you prefer yours drier, just let it cook a bit longer.

Buckwheat Crêpes with Spinach-Dill Scramble

Makes about 10 crêpes

I met Geoff Clevenger when I worked for cookbook author and French cooking-school owner *extraordinaire* Susan Hermann Loomis. A fellow Francophile and unabashed punster, he's the creative cook who developed this recipe. Nowadays, Geoff's vocation combines his talents in marketing and advertising with web application design, and I'm very lucky he's in charge of my site.

Crêpes

2 large eggs, beaten lightly

2/3 cup milk

2/3 cup water

1/2 teaspoon salt

2 tablespoons canola oil, plus 1 tablespoon for oiling pan

1/2 cup buckwheat flour

1/2 cup white flour

In a medium-sized bowl, combine all of the ingredients except for the flours. Then add the flours and whisk until smooth. Pour through a fine mesh sieve and stir to blend. Let the batter sit at least 1 hour before using. It can be made a day ahead and refrigerated. Before using, give the batter a good stir to blend.

Heat to medium-hot a sturdy 10-inch skillet. Lightly oil the skillet with an oiled paper towel and pour in about 3 tablespoons of the batter, swirling the skillet to spread the batter evenly. (You *may* have to add some flour or water to get the batter to a consistency that is neither too thin nor too thick, but try it first without.)

Cook until the edges start to curl and the crepe is lightly browned, about 1 1/2 to 2 minutes. Turn over and cook another 30 seconds to 1 minute. Be prepared to throw the first couple of crêpes away until you get the temperature just right. Or, if they're only cosmetically challenged, eat them right out of the pan with a little butter, a little jam, and a little powdered sugar.

You can make these a day ahead and store in the refrigerator wrapped tightly in plastic wrap. They also freeze well.

Filling   Makes 5 to 6 crêpe bundles

1 bunch fresh spinach, stems removed (leaves without stems weigh about 9 ounces), washed, and cut into 1-inch ribbons

1 tablespoon canola oil

6 large eggs

1 tablespoon fresh chopped dill

2 tablespoons water

³/₄ teaspoon salt

Freshly ground pepper

2 tablespoons olive oil

5 ounces goat cheese, cut into small cubes

About 2 tablespoons Crème Fraîche (page 135) or sour cream

Sprigs of dill

Heat a large sauté pan over medium-high heat, add the canola oil and then the spinach. Cook for about 2 minutes, stirring, until just tender. Remove from heat, transfer spinach to a strainer, and let drain while you continue. Press the spinach a couple of times to remove excess liquid.

Beat together the egg, dill, water, salt, and pepper. Heat a sauté pan to medium-hot with the olive oil, and when the oil is hot but not smoking, pour in the egg mixture. Stir gently until the mixture is thickened but still quite wet. Add the goat cheese and spinach, and continue cooking until the eggs are fully set and the cheese begins to melt.

Divide the egg mixture among 6 warm crêpes, fold, and serve. For an attractive presentation, make a small bundle with each crêpe, and on the less presentable side (the second side cooked), place a portion of the cooked eggs and spinach in the center. Fold the sides in toward the middle, as with a blintz, and nimbly flip over. Garnish with a dab of crème fraîche and a sprig of dill. Great with fried potatoes and a fruit salad.

EGGS

Kaiserschmarren
(The Emperor's Omelette)
82

Summertime Omelette
83

Blue Cheese, Bacon, Apple
& Walnut Omelette
84

Andouille Omelette Filling
86

Bacon & Goat Cheese
Omelette Filling
87

Chicken Liver Omelette Filling
88

Cherry Omelette
89

Joana's Frittata
90

Noodle Frittata
91

Merry Christmas Frittata
92

Persian Eggs
93

Catalan Omelette Cake
(Pastel de Truita)
94

Huevos Rancheros
96

Spinach Soufflé
97

Ole Souffle
99

Salzburger Nockerl
100

Egg & Onion Fried Matzo,
aka Matzo Brei
101

Mendocino Frittata
102

Kaiserschmarren (The Emperor's Omelette)

Makes 4 servings

Once I discovered this Austrian specialty, a favorite food of Emperor Franz Josef's, I embarked upon a mission to taste it in as many restaurants in Austria as possible. And it was delicious everywhere. I love the egginess of the thick, puffy pancake. And with the addition of fruit, sautéed or as a compote, it's a complete meal. One variation calls for caramelized apple slices added at the same time as the raisins, giving an additional hint of sweetness.

1/4 cup raisins

1/4 cup dark rum (or Austrian Stroh rum, if you are lucky enough to find it)

4 egg yolks

1/4 cup sugar

1/4 teaspoon salt

2 cups whole milk

1/4 teaspoon vanilla

1 cup white flour

4 egg whites

4 tablespoons unsalted butter

Powdered sugar

2 cups lingonberry or plum compote, or applesauce

In a small pot, bring raisins and rum to a boil; remove from heat and cover. Set aside for at least 30 minutes, then drain. The leftover rum is a small bonus for the cook.

In a mixing bowl, blend together egg yolks, sugar, salt, milk, vanilla, and flour until smooth.

In a separate bowl, beat whites until stiff, but not dry. Fold whites into the very thin batter.

Melt 1/2 tablespoon butter in a 10-inch nonstick sauté pan over high heat, pour in about 1 1/2 cups of the batter, turn heat down to medium, and cook for about 4 minutes, until the underside is golden brown. Peek to make sure it is not getting too brown.

While cooking, sprinkle a quarter of the raisins over the uncooked surface. Slide the pancake out onto a warmed plate, add 1/2 tablespoon butter to the pan, quickly melt, and invert the pancake back into the pan. Continue cooking for 3 to 4 minutes.

Using two forks, tear the pancake into several small pieces (yes, you are "destroying" your creation!). Toss back into the pan for another couple of minutes to dry out.

Slide out onto a warm plate and sift powdered sugar generously over the top. Serve immediately with a side of compote or applesauce. Repeat procedure for additional servings.

Summertime Omelette

Makes 1 omelette

You can make this omelette, as I do, using whatever vegetables that happen to be in the refrigerator: carrots, spinach, zucchini, mushrooms, bell peppers, green onions. It is hard to think of a vegetable that wouldn't work. You may think this is a lot of ingredients to combine with only two eggs, but the quantities are fairly small and the volume reduces when sautéed.

Filling

2 teaspoons olive or canola oil,
  or unsalted butter

$1/2$ cup (or a bit more) thinly
  sliced vegetables

Salt

Pepper

2 cherry tomatoes, cut in half

Omelette

2 large eggs

1 teaspoon cold water

3 drops Tabasco sauce

2 teaspoons unsalted butter,
  or 1 teaspoon butter and
  1 teaspoon canola oil

1 teaspoon finely chopped fresh
  herbs: your choice of tarragon,
  basil, oregano, chervil, dill,
  or cilantro

1 ounce grated cheese (I enjoy a
  medium-sharp Cheddar)

Place an 8-inch nonstick pan over medium heat, add the oil or butter and when warm, add the $1/2$ cup vegetables, tossing with a wooden spatula until they are tender but not limp. Spinach should be added only in the last 20 seconds. Season with salt and pepper, remove from the pan, and set aside.

Wipe the pan with a paper towel. With a fork, beat together the eggs, water, and Tabasco sauce until blended. Again, heat the pan over medium heat, add the butter or oil, then the herbs, and immediately pour in the beaten eggs. Let sit on the heat for 5 seconds. Then, holding the panhandle, slowly start to swirl the egg mixture in the pan, distributing the herbs evenly.

With a wooden spatula, pull the outside of the eggs toward the center, tilting the pan to allow the uncooked egg to spill into the pan. When the eggs have set, you can flip them if you're feeling adventuresome, or not if you're not. This also depends on how soft-cooked you like your eggs.

To fill, distribute the cheese quickly in a line down the center of the omelette. Follow with the cooked vegetables and the tomatoes.

Slowly slide the omelette onto a heated plate until about half is on the plate and half is still in the pan. Then, using the pan to help, fold the other half of the omelette over the top of the portion that is already on the plate.

Blue Cheese, Bacon, Apple & Walnut Omelette

Makes 1 omelette

I like to combine eggs with cheese and fruit and, of course, the saltiness and smokiness of the bacon goes well with the tanginess of the blue cheese. Under other circumstances, the apple would be too much, but in this dish it comes between the blue cheese and the bacon, preventing any competition of flavors.

It could be argued that the eggs are almost incidental to this omelette; they just lend credence to the filling, while holding the whole works together. When making an omelette, I always try to put the cheese in first, right on the egg, to give it a chance to melt, or at least to soften. I especially like the Maytag brand of blue cheese, but any good blue cheese will do.

Filling

1 ounce blue cheese

1 tablespoon sour cream

2 tablespoons toasted walnuts, coarsely chopped and tossed in a sieve for about 30 seconds to remove as much of the "skin" as possible; the walnut hair or fuzz or whatever it's called sticks to the sieve, leaving you with neatly naked little walnuts

1/6 to 1/4 of a green apple, thinly sliced

4 teaspoons butter

2 tablespoons cooked crumbled bacon

Omelette

2 large eggs

2 teaspoons cold water

2 drops Tabasco sauce

Mix the blue cheese, sour cream, and walnuts, and set aside. Sauté the apple slices in 2 teaspoons of the butter just until soft, about 3 minutes, and set aside. Have the crumbled bacon handy.

Beat the eggs together with the water and Tabasco sauce until the yolks and whites are blended. Do not overbeat. Heat an 8-inch pan (I use Silverstone exclusively, because it *never* sticks) until it is quite hot and add the remaining 2 teaspoons butter (it should sizzle). In the next few seconds, pour the eggs into the pan.

Start rotating the pan over the heat to form a cohesive mass. You can help this along by pushing the outside of the eggs toward the center of the pan with a wooden spatula. The instant the eggs are no longer liquid, layer in the filling down the center: first the blue cheese mixture, then the sautéed apples, and then the crumbled bacon. Fold, and serve immediately on a warm plate.

I flip the eggs so the top becomes the bottom and then I add the filling. It depends on how creamy you prefer the eggs; they are creamier when cooked only on one side.

Andouille Omelette Filling

Makes enough for 4 to 6 omelettes

This was the best-selling omelette at the restaurant on Sundays. Customers went wild for it. We could have made it by the cement-truck full.

1 medium eggplant (about
    1 pound), diced into $1/2$-inch
    cubes (skin can be left on)

3 tablespoons olive oil

1 medium zucchini, sliced length-
    wise, then in $1/4$-inch half
    circles

1 teaspoon minced garlic

8 ounces andouille sausage links,
    baked or poached, allowed to
    cool, then sliced

$1/3$ cup Herbed Cream Cheese
    (page 135)

1 tomato, chopped

3 tablespoons toasted pine nuts

Salt

Freshly ground pepper

Preheat the oven to 350°F.

Mix together eggplant and 2 tablespoons of the olive oil, spread into a 9- by 13-inch baking pan, and season with salt. Bake for about 30 to 40 minutes, stirring occasionally to prevent sticking. Remove when soft and slightly brown.

Sauté the zucchini in the remaining 1 tablespoon of olive oil over medium heat until soft, add garlic, and continue cooking for 1 minute. Season with salt and pepper, and add to eggplant. In the same pan, sauté the sausage until brown. Mix together all the ingredients and taste for seasoning.

If the filling needs to be reheated, pop it in a 375°F oven for 5 to 7 minutes.

Flipping Omelettes

The only "secret" to making omelettes is flipping them. Move the pan a certain way, and the arc that you create forces the omelette to obey. It's a matter of practice, which a lot of people seem reluctant to do because they think "practicing" is a waste of ingredients. But consider this: Set aside half an hour and three dozen eggs. That will give you 18 two-egg omelettes to flip. Even if you have a string of disas-ters (for which your dog will love you!), you'll achieve success for less than $10, which is considerably less than the price of a gourmet cooking class. So make the investment, wait until no one is around to snicker, spread a plastic tarp on the floor, and go for it. It's like learning to swim or ride a bike. Somewhere between the third and twelfth try, you'll get it.

Bacon & Goat Cheese Omelette Filling

Makes enough for 4 omelettes

I usually use a combination of greens, depending on what's available locally. And we use Laura Chenel's California Chèvre; it's just goaty enough to be interesting but not overwhelming.

6 strips (8, if skinny) uncooked bacon, diced

1 cup finely chopped leeks or green onions

3 tablespoons olive oil

1 teaspoon minced garlic

5 cups spinach, chard, bok choy, beet greens, kale, or any other green that can be cooked and cut into ribbons (stack the leaves and cut into strips 3/4-inch wide; include the stems if they're tender)

Salt

Freshly ground pepper

8 ounces goat cheese

2 tablespoons sour cream

Fry the bacon until done and drain. Sauté the leeks or onions in olive oil until just tender. Add the garlic to the pan, then the greens, and sauté over medium heat until tender and reduced. (The greens will deflate dramatically, by as much as 75 percent.) Remove from heat and season with salt and pepper. Crumble the goat cheese and mix in. If the mixture seems dry, add sour cream. Heat the filling for 5 minutes in a 375°F oven before using in omelettes.

Bringing Home the Bacon

Restaurants cook their bacon on racks in the oven to simplify the process. Rather than having to dodge splattering bacon fat on the top of the stove, separate strips of raw bacon and lay them side-by-side on a cake rack. Place the rack on a pan with sides in a 325°F oven. Check after about 12 to 15 minutes. Not cooked enough for you? Leave it in the oven another 5 to 10 minutes. Remove when done to your liking and let cool. Rewarm briefly in the oven before serving.

Chicken Liver Omelette Filling

Makes enough for 4 omelettes

When I first came to Mendocino in 1975 and ate at Cafe Beaujolais (with no notion that one day I would own it!), I often ordered the Pitsenbargers' chicken liver omelette, which was very good, and one of the few things I could then afford.

You may not be filled with enthusiasm about performing surgery on the chicken livers, but it is essential in order to prevent bitterness and an odd texture, so grit your teeth and do it. No big deal, and the result is well worth it.

2 medium yellow onions (about 1^1/$_2$ pounds), minced

6 tablespoons butter

2 teaspoons salt

2 teaspoons fresh sage or marjoram, chopped

6 chicken livers (about 12 ounces, the palest available)

Freshly ground pepper

^{1}/$_3$ cup port, sherry, or Madeira

Sauté the onions in butter with a big pinch of salt over very low heat for about 25 minutes, until golden brown and cooked all the way through. Drain, and set the onions aside in a bowl, reserving the butter. Add the herb of your choice to the onions and stir.

Wash the livers and remove membranes and any green spots. Pat them dry and season both sides with the remaining salt and some pepper. Pour the butter back into the pan, turn the heat to high, and sauté the livers for about 1^1/$_2$ minutes on each side to brown evenly. With a slotted spoon, remove the livers from the pan and add them to the onions. Pour off the fat from the pan, place the pan over high heat, and, within a few seconds, add the port. Cook to reduce, scraping the bottom of the pan until only 1 or 2 syrupy tablespoons are left. Pour over the liver and onion mixture and gently combine.

Cherry Omelette

Makes 1 serving

Many years ago, soon after I took over the restaurant, a Swiss gentleman on staff at Cafe Beaujolais for a few months happened to mention that cherry omelettes were quite popular in Switzerland. I must have filed that information away in some deep recess of my brain, because it came back to me once, when cherries were just coming into season. I decided to add the sugar and vanilla, to make it unlike any ordinary omelette, more like a breakfast dessert, and I think it is exceptionally delicious. It's not so sweet that it is really peculiar—just unusual. I would serve it with muffins or toast. My only warning is to exercise care when pitting and chopping the cherries to keep the juice from getting under your fingernails. I lived with this recipe for a week and a half, despite frequent scrubbings.

The recipe does work with other fruits, especially berries, but it doesn't have the same special texture or quality that cherries bring to it.

Omelette

2 large eggs

2 teaspoons sugar

$1/8$ teaspoon vanilla extract

1 teaspoon butter

Filling

$1/2$ cup pitted fresh cherries, coarsely chopped

1 tablespoon sour cream

Beat together the eggs, sugar, and vanilla. In a small nonstick pan, heat the cherries quickly until warm. In another nonstick pan, heat the butter until it foams, then add the eggs and make an omelette. When the eggs are set, add the sour cream and then the warm cherries. Fold and serve.

Joana's Frittata

Makes 2 to 3 servings

Joana Bryar-Matons was a marvelous cook whose "Catalan Baked Fish" in my first book, *Cafe Beaujolais*, is beloved by many. She grew up in Barcelona, where one develops a special appreciation for the magic you can do with olive oil, vegetables, and eggs.

1 tablespoon olive oil

1/4 cup finely chopped green onions

1/4 cup thinly sliced mushrooms

1/4 cup diced bell peppers (a combination of colors looks especially nice)

1/4 cup peeled and seeded tomatoes (or the equivalent in unpeeled, unseeded cherry tomatoes)

Salt

Freshly ground black pepper

1 teaspoon finely chopped fresh basil, oregano, or marjoram

1 tablespoon minced fresh parsley

4 large eggs

1/4 teaspoon Tabasco sauce

1 cup grated cheese of your choice

1 tablespoon grated dry cheese (Parmesan, dry Jack, dry Asiago)

In a 10-inch nonstick pan, heat the olive oil and add the onion, mushrooms, and bell peppers. Over medium heat, sauté until soft. Add the tomatoes and sauté for another minute or so. Season with salt and pepper, and add the fresh herbs.

Beat eggs with Tabasco sauce and pour over the vegetables. Sprinkle the cheeses over the surface. Cover with a tight-fitting lid and reduce the heat to the lowest possible level. Cook for about 5 to 8 minutes, until set and firm, then serve immediately.

Noodle Frittata

Makes 1 serving

While assembling the recipes for this book, it was suggested to me that I should include a section entitled "Around the World with Fried Starch." Can I help it if the restaurant clientele had a fondness for carbohydrates? We had many celebrity customers over the years, but I don't think Dr. Atkins ever dined with us.

I devised this recipe strictly on the basis of what sounded good to me. Noodles and eggs seemed to put a slight ethnic tilt on the matzo and eggs dish in my first book. Imagine my surprise when my mother, browsing through her vast collection of cookbooks, discovered an old Italian recipe for Frittata a la Spaghettini. You guessed it: noodles and eggs. I say "noodles" and not "pasta" because the word noodles sounds more down-to-earth. Pasta is trendy; noodles are not. This is one of the few egg dishes that I prefer well done and browned on the outside. If you don't want it this way, you will need to adjust the timing.

1/2 cup finely chopped onions

1 tablespoon olive oil

2 ounces pasta (your choice of shape), cooked, drained, and chilled

Salt

Freshly ground black pepper

2 large eggs, beaten

1 tablespoon grated dry cheese

In an 8-inch nonstick pan, heat the oil and add the onions. Sauté until golden. Lift the onions from the pan, leaving the oil. Add the noodles. Season with salt and pepper, cook over medium heat until golden brown and crunchy, then add the cooked onions. Season the eggs and pour them into the pan, covering the noodles. Sprinkle the cheese over the surface of the eggs.

Cover the pan with a lid and reduce the heat to low. Cook for about 1 minute, then remove the lid and flip, either by nimbly tossing the frittata in the air, or by placing a plate over the pan, turning the whole works upside down, and sliding the frittata back into the pan. Cook for another minute or so, and serve.

Merry Christmas Frittata

Makes 3 to 4 servings

It's "Merry Christmas" because of the red and green peppers. Oddly enough, the recipe was developed for *Chocolatier* magazine. The editors wanted a whole bunch of chocolate recipes, of course, but they also wanted something that wasn't sweet and that anyone could make from basic ingredients you can get anywhere.

A frittata can be served hot or cold or anywhere in between, and at any time of the day. At the restaurant, we used to serve this hot in the early morning and at room temperature later in the day, because most people associate breakfast with hot food, although I think this dish tastes best at room temperature. To forestall complaints, our wait staff explained to customers that we *meant* to serve it at room temperature.

1 tablespoon unsalted butter melted with 1 tablespoon olive oil

1/2 cup finely chopped red onions

1/2 cup chopped fresh green chiles (as hot as you desire)

3/4 cup chopped roasted red peppers

3 tablespoons grated dry cheese (Parmesan, dry Jack, or dry Asiago)

Salt

Freshly ground black pepper

1/2 teaspoon fresh, finely chopped oregano

1/2 teaspoon Tabasco sauce

8 large eggs, beaten

Avocado slices and/or sour cream, for garnish

Preheat the oven to 350°F.

Grease an 8-inch square pan with some of the butter-oil mixture and set aside.

Put the remaining butter-oil in a small nonstick pan and sauté the onions over medium heat, until they are softened but not brown. Add the chiles and cook for another 2 minutes. Set aside and let cool.

Mix the onions and chiles together with all the remaining ingredients, except for the garnish.

Pour into the pan and bake for 30 minutes, until the top is slightly brown. Serve at any temperature you wish, garnished as indicated above.

Persian Eggs

Makes 2 servings

This is another recipe from Anni Amberger (Mocha Walnut Wonder Muffins, page 24), although as far as I know, it was never served to Stevie Wonder. It's a baked egg dish with a very nice blend of flavors that comes out quite differently depending on whether you use curry or saffron. The presentation on a bed of vegetables creates interesting textures and flavors. Although it seems quite intricate, it is really easy to put together.

When I was testing the recipe, I tended to overbake the eggs, which isn't terrible, but it's better when the whites are firm and the yolks are runny. So be careful. You may want to prepare this once or twice before serving it to guests.

You can also use two ovenproof baking dishes instead of the pan if you wish to make individual servings.

2 tablespoons olive oil

2 tomatoes, peeled and chopped

1/2 cup finely chopped onion

1/2 cup finely chopped green peppers

1/2 cup finely chopped mushrooms

1 teaspoon minced garlic

1/4 teaspoon Beaujolais Blend Herbs* or dried oregano

1/2 teaspoon curry powder or 2 pinches saffron

3 tablespoons lemon juice

Salt

Freshly ground black pepper

4 large eggs

2 tablespoons grated dry cheese (Parmesan, dry Monterey Jack, Asiago)

1/2 cup grated cheese (Monterey Jack, Cheddar, or Swiss)

Chopped parsley or cilantro for topping

* Beaujolais Blend Herbs are available from Fuller's Fine Herbs (www.fullersfineherbs.com)

Preheat the oven to 350°F.

In a large ovenproof frying pan, heat the oil and sauté the tomatoes, onion, pepper, mushrooms, and garlic for 3 minutes. Add the herbs, spice, lemon juice, and salt and pepper to taste, and cook for 1 more minute.

Smooth out the vegetables and make four evenly-spaced depressions on the vegetable bed. Carefully crack an egg into each depression and sprinkle with the cheeses.

Place the frying pan in the oven for 12 to 15 minutes, until the eggs are just set. Serve immediately, sprinkled with chopped parsley or cilantro.

Catalan Omelette Cake (Pastel de Truita)

Makes 6 to 8 servings

This is the omelette equivalent of *pousse café*, a remarkable creation comprised of four separate frittatas (frittatae?) layered with tomato and eggplant sauce. Actually, it's my interpretation of pages and pages of almost-impossible-to-read script that arrived years ago from my Spanish friend, Joana Bryar-Matons. The two very clear things that can be said about it are:

1. It is incredibly messy to make, and
2. It is worth it.

In Joana's version, the finished cake is "frosted" with mayonnaise, but this sounded so bizarre to me that I didn't even try it, although you are more than welcome to do so. I choose to cover mine with more of the tomato and eggplant sauce and some fresh herbs. You may add other ingredients to any or all of the layers: mushrooms, other vegetables, and so forth. Serve it at room temperature.

12 large eggs

1/2 teaspoon Tabasco sauce

About 6 tablespoons olive oil

1 medium red potato, peeled, and cut into matchstick-sized pieces

Salt

Pepper

1/4 cup grated dry cheese (Parmesan, dry Jack, dry Asiago)

2 cups spinach leaves, cut into ribbons

1 cup quartered marinated artichoke hearts, drained

1 1/2 cups cooked salted white beans

1 teaspoon minced garlic

2 tablespoons minced fresh parsley

2 cups Tomato-Eggplant Sauce (page 136)

Beat the eggs with the Tabasco sauce, and divide into four equal parts.

For the potato omelette layer: In a 10-inch nonstick pan, heat 2 tablespoons of the oil and add potato sticks when the oil is hot but not smoking.

Toss the potatoes until they are soft and slightly brown. Season with salt and pepper.

With the pan over medium heat, add 1 portion of eggs and mix the potatoes in quickly so they are evenly distributed.

Reduce the heat to very low, sprinkle with 1 tablespoon of the cheese, and cover with a tight-fitting lid. Cook until the eggs are no longer runny, about 3 minutes. Slide the omelette onto a flat surface and keep warm.

For the spinach omelette layer: Heat 1 tablespoon oil in the pan and add the spinach, stirring and tossing until it has reduced significantly and is tender, about 45 seconds. Season with salt and pepper. Increase the heat and add 1 portion of eggs, mixing to distribute the spinach evenly. Reduce heat to very low, sprinkle with 1 tablespoon cheese, and cover with a tight-fitting lid.

Cook until the eggs are no longer runny, about 3 minutes. Slide the omelette onto a flat surface and keep warm.

For the artichoke layer: Add the artichokes to the pan and heat. Season with salt and pepper. Add 1 teaspoon of the oil, one portion of the eggs, and 1 tablespoon of the cheese. Cover the pan, allowing the eggs to cook until they are no longer runny, about 4 minutes. Slide the omelette onto a flat surface and keep warm.

For the white bean omelette layer: Heat 2 tablespoons oil in the pan and add the cooked beans, garlic, and parsley. Over low heat, cook about 3 minutes. Try not to mash the beans. Season with pepper. Add the last portion of eggs and mix gently to distribute evenly. Sprinkle with 1 tablespoon cheese.

Cover with the lid and cook, over low heat, for 3 minutes. Slide out onto your serving plate, which should be completely flat.

To assemble the cake: Gently mash the warm Tomato-Eggplant Sauce so that there are no pieces of eggplant to create lumps in your "cake." Transfer the white bean layer onto the serving dish you plan to use. Measure slightly less than a quarter of the sauce onto the middle of the white bean layer. Spread evenly all the way to the edges. Carefully position the artichoke layer onto the top of the sauce. Add more sauce, then the spinach layer, then more sauce, and then the potato layer. Add the remaining sauce, using it to cover the top and sides, as if you were frosting a cake. Sprinkle with parsley and cut into wedges to serve.

Huevos Rancheros

Makes 1 serving

I thought about renaming this dish, but Huevos Rancheros is what it is. Instead of frying the eggs, I poach them in the salsa, and they come out truly delicious. Occasionally, the eggs will stick to the bottom of the pan; if this happens to you, run a rubber spatula gently under the egg to loosen. Be forewarned that dawdling during this recipe results in hard-cooked eggs. Prepare yourself for precision timing because the whole thing comes together in about 3 minutes. And for the salsa, either use the recipe in this book or purchase your favorite prepared commercial brand. To make this for more than one person, increase the salsa by about $1/4$ cup per additional serving.

1 cup salsa

2 large eggs

2 corn tortillas or 1 large flour tortilla (10 to 12 inches in diameter)

$1/4$ to $1/2$ cup grated Monterey Jack or Cheddar cheese

About $3/4$ cup Black Bean Chili (page 153), heated

About $1/2$ cup shredded crunchy lettuce (optional)

1 tablespoon chopped black olives

Sour cream

Chopped cilantro

In a small frying pan, heat the salsa to near boiling. Break each egg into a separate small bowl and gently add to the salsa. Cover the pan and cook over low heat for about 3 minutes, occasionally spooning sauce over the eggs, and checking to be sure the eggs aren't sticking to the bottom of the pan.

Heat the tortilla(s) either on a skillet on top of the stove or in a 350°F oven. Sprinkle the cheese evenly over the surface of the tortilla(s) and let it melt. Remove from heat and spread with chili. If you're using lettuce, arrange it around the edge of the tortilla.

With a large spoon, carefully remove the eggs from the salsa and place in the middle of your creation. Spoon salsa over the top and garnish with olives, sour cream, and cilantro. Serve immediately.

Spinach Soufflé

Makes 5 to 6 servings

The word "soufflé" was a catchall term at the restaurant for dishes that we weren't quite sure how to identify. For some reason, customers were more likely to order a soufflé, rather than a pudding or casserole, thus making the name a marketing decision as well.

While I prefer fresh vegetables most of the time, this recipe works well with frozen spinach. I would serve it hot or warm, for breakfast, brunch, a light supper, on a picnic— gosh, it's so good, you'll wonder how you've lived this long without it!

1 cup finely chopped onions

2 tablespoons olive oil or butter

2 teaspoons minced garlic

1 (10-ounce) package frozen chopped spinach, defrosted, and squeezed dry

1 cup grated dry cheese (Parmesan, dry Asiago, or dry Jack)

1/2 cup ricotta cheese

4 large eggs, separated, plus 1 additional white

1 teaspoon Beaujolais Blend Herbs* or dried oregano

1/4 teaspoon freshly grated nutmeg

3/4 teaspoon salt

1/4 teaspoon freshly ground black pepper

White Sauce

2 tablespoons unsalted butter

2 tablespoons white flour

1 1/2 cups warm milk

* Beaujolais Blend Herbs are available from Fuller's Fine Herbs (www.fullersfineherbs.com)

Preheat oven to 375°F.

Sauté the onions in oil or butter over medium heat for about 10 minutes until golden brown. Add the garlic and spinach and cook briefly, about 1 minute longer. Transfer to a large bowl, allow to cool, then add the cheeses, egg yolks, herbs, nutmeg, salt, and pepper, and stir to combine. Set aside.

To make the white sauce: Over medium heat, melt the butter in a pan and add the flour, stirring for 3 minutes without browning. Add the milk and stir for 5 minutes more; the sauce should be thick and smooth.

Cool to tepid and add to the spinach mixture.

Beat the egg whites until stiff, but not dry.

Stir about a quarter of the whites into the spinach mixture to lighten it, then fold in the remaining whites.

Pour into a buttered 8-inch square pan (or any baking dish with a 6- to 8-cup capacity) and bake for 35 to 45 minutes. Serve immediately or at any temperature desired.

This is delicious reheated and, in that case, its name changes to Soufflé Replay (or, perhaps, Replé).

Ole Souffle

Makes 2 to 4 servings

Notice the absence of accent marks on the recipe title. That's because it is pronounced "OH-lee SOOF-ull," who may have been the Norwegian sea captain who first . . . (oh, never mind). Would you be more likely to order Pudding? See. It does have egg whites folded in, so the French Soufflé Acceptance Board might at least take our application. But it also has some lovely Latin touches that make the finished product spicy and delicious.

Ole Souffle can be a side dish with Black Bean Chili (page 153) or vice versa, or an entrée all on its own, with fresh fruit or a green salad on the side.

3/4 cup creamed corn

2 large eggs, separated

2 tablespoons canola oil

1/2 cup milk

3/4 cup cornmeal

1/2 teaspoon salt

1/2 teaspoon baking soda

4 ounces (1 generous cup) grated extra sharp Cheddar cheese

1 to 2 tablespoons finely chopped fresh jalapeño chiles

Topping

Sour cream

Salsa

Chopped green or finely diced red onions

Cilantro

Preheat the oven to 350°F.

Combine the corn, egg yolks, oil, and milk. In a separate bowl, mix cornmeal, salt, and baking soda, and add to the liquids, mixing well. Beat egg whites until stiff, but not dry, and fold in quickly.

Pour half of the mixture into a greased 8-inch square pan, sprinkle evenly with the cheese and chiles. Pour the remaining batter over, smooth to cover, and bake for about 30 minutes. Test for doneness with a knife inserted in the center. If it emerges clean, the soufflé is done. Let cool on a rack for 3 to 5 minutes. It will deflate slightly. Serve with the desired toppings.

Salzburger Nockerl

Makes 2 to 3 servings

I have a greater appreciation for this recipe since living in Austria, where the culinary culture is permeated with delicious dishes made from ingredients with little or no redeeming nutritional value. I like that. So many Austrian specialties are rich and sweet and made to eat with a cup of delicious strong coffee, and that's that, no excuses. The butter, the eggs, the chocolate, the nuts—all are combined in the most glorious ways. Nockerl, one of the most famous Austrian desserts, is a sort of soufflé omelette that has its origins in the so-called "plain" cooking of the nineteenth century. Yes, this fluffy bit of madness was considered plain cooking! As with the Kaiserschmarren (page 82), one is cautioned to *not* eat it after a big meal, or better yet, to consider it the meal in its entirety. Ah, *yes*, a country that encourages dessert for the entrée!

My dear friend Stephanie Kroninger retrieved this recipe from her family files and shared it with me before her untimely death in 1993.

1 1/2 tablespoons clarified butter

3 egg yolks

2 tablespoons white flour

Zest from 1 lemon

1/2 teaspoon vanilla

4 egg whites

1/4 teaspoon cream of tartar

1/8 teaspoon salt

1/3 cup white sugar

Powdered sugar for garnish, if desired

Preheat the oven to 350°F.

Melt the butter in a 10-inch ovenproof pan (I use cast iron). Set aside.

In a small bowl, gently mix together with a fork the egg yolks, flour, lemon zest, and vanilla. Set aside.

Beat the egg whites with the cream of tartar and salt until soft peaks form. Gradually beat in the sugar, 1 tablespoon at a time. Continue beating until the whites form stiff peaks (when you remove the beaters, the whites will stand straight up in the bowl).

Stir about a quarter of the whites into the yolks to lighten. Pour the mixture over the remaining whites and fold in with a large rubber spatula. Traditionally, the batter is placed in the pan in 3 or 4 mounds. I have also poured the batter into the pan and baked it as one piece.

In any case, bake for about 10 to 13 minutes, until the top is very golden brown. Remove and serve immediately. This dish is already sweet enough, but it is usually served with powdered sugar lightly sifted over the top.

Egg & Onion Fried Matzo, aka Matzo Brei

Makes 2 servings

I seem to spend a lot of time discussing fried matzo with friends. Noted local architect, and one of the most creative cooks I know, Michael Leventhal, gave me his recipe, which I've embellished a bit. If we're lucky, in my next book he'll share his astonishing Tomato & Bread Salad (made with grilled pizza crust).

1 tablespoon unsalted butter

¼ cup minced red onions

½ teaspoon minced garlic

3 Egg and Onion Matzo crackers, broken into roughly 1- to 2-inch pieces

2 large eggs

2 tablespoons milk

2 teaspoons fresh dill, chopped

Salt

Freshly ground pepper

Heat a small pan over low heat, add 2 teaspoons butter and onion. Cook onions until tender and slightly browned.

Remove from heat, add garlic, and cover, allowing it to "cook" in the residual heat.

Place matzo pieces in a bowl. Pour warm water over them and drain immediately.

Start to heat a 10-inch nonstick pan while beating eggs with milk, dill, salt, and pepper. Add egg mixture to drained matzo, stir well, add remaining butter to the hot pan, and turn up heat. Immediately pour egg mixture into the pan, add onions and garlic, and stir constantly. The cooking is done when the eggs and matzo are on the drier side, not creamy.

Serve immediately with extra salt and pepper.

The School of Hard Knock-Erls: Reflections on Recipe Authenticity

Before anyone contacts me about the authenticity of the recipes in this book, I want to say this: "I know already. I make no claims. Bottom line: Good-tasting food is what's important to me." And even the most traditional dish seems to have a great many versions. Each era, each region, each family, puts a particular twist on what they like to eat. My curiosity led me to an Internet search on Salzburger Nockerl, and I was amazed to see the range of amounts of ingredients in the many recipes I scanned. For 4 yolks, sometimes as many as 9 whites are used, sometimes as few as 4. Sometimes whipping cream even finds its way in (I think there are Austrians who will put *Schlag* in anything). Temperatures rose to 450°F or plummeted to 325°F. People, this is an *enormous* difference. Unless you are trying to reproduce The Real Thing (which is very hard to pin down) for a specific reason, spend your efforts coming up with the version(s) you like the best. Then you can turn others on to The New and Improved recipe, and everyone will think you are a creative genius.

Mendocino Frittata

Makes 8 servings

A classic frittata that allows for infinite variations. Perfect for any meal, any time.

9 large eggs

2 tablespoons minced parsley

1/4 cup grated dry cheese
   (Parmesan, dry Asiago, or
   dry Jack)

Salt

Freshly ground pepper

1 1/4 cups cubed (3/4-inch) cooked,
   peeled potatoes

3 to 4 tablespoons olive oil

3/4 cup finely chopped red peppers

2/3 cup finely chopped green
   onions

2 teaspoons fresh thyme leaves

1/4 teaspoon cayenne pepper

3 ounces goat cheese, cut into
   small cubes or thin slices,
   depending on shape

1/2 cup cherry tomatoes, cut in
   half

1/4 cup roasted garlic

Beat eggs with parsley, dry cheese, salt, and freshly ground pepper. Set aside.

Heat a large ovenproof sauté pan, add olive oil, and cook potatoes over medium heat until well browned on all sides, about 10 minutes.

Add peppers and sauté until soft.

Add green onions, cook until limp, and add thyme.

Sprinkle cayenne pepper over vegetables and stir to distribute. (Turn on the broiler at this point.)

Turn up the heat and add egg mixture.

Turn heat down to medium-low. Quickly place goat cheese, cherry tomatoes, and roasted garlic evenly over the surface.

Reduce the heat to low and let cook, slowly, until the edges are set. Lift the edges so that uncooked egg can run underneath, and repeat this a couple of times during the next 5 minutes or so. Peek underneath and make sure the bottom isn't browning too quickly. If it is, reduce heat.

When the top is set and still moist, place the pan under the broiler for 45 to 60 seconds, until the top is slightly browned. Slide frittata out onto a warmed dish and cut into wedges.

To roast the garlic: In a saucepan, place peeled garlic and cover with water. Bring to a boil and lower heat. Simmer for 5 to 7 minutes until easily pierced with the tip of a knife. Drain well.

Coat the cloves with a generous amount of olive oil and bake at 325°F for about 20 to 25 minutes, stirring occasionally, until caramelized. Store in the refrigerator, covered in oil.

SANDWICHES & SOUPS

Creamy Mozzarella Sandwich
106

Egg Salad Sandwich
107

Open-faced Smoked Salmon
Sandwich
108

Smoked Turkey Salad Sandwich
109

Chicken Stock
110

Grandma Kump's Asparagus,
Tarragon & Garlic Soup
111

Posole
112

Spinach & Mint Soup
113

Roasted Butternut Squash Soup
115

Cold Fusion Soup
117

Creamy Mozzarella Sandwich

Makes 1 serving

This started out as a lunch item, but because we eat bread in the morning and we eat cheese in the morning, it is entirely appropriate to combine them in this attractive and versatile sandwich. At the restaurant, we used to serve it about three times a week, grilled and then baked. It can be open-faced or closed-faced. It is especially nice with black olives and sliced tomatoes drizzled with vinaigrette.

Purchase mozzarella that is not rubbery. As you only need two ounces per serving, why not splurge and buy the very best you can find?

1 slice good-quality bread, toasted (I like to use an herb bread or whole wheat)

About 2 teaspoons Pesto (page 141) or an olive spread, such as tapenade or olivada

About 2 teaspoons diced or puréed dried tomatoes in olive oil

About 1 to 2 ounces whole milk mozzarella, grated

Spread the pesto over one side of the bread, then spread the tomatoes over it. Sprinkle the mozzarella over the surface all the way to the edges so that every bite has all three ingredients.

Broil, until the cheese is melted, and enjoy.

A Philosophical Tizzy

As I wondered whether or not to include such a simple recipe in this book, I started to think about what cooking is really all about. Does it have to involve transformation, so that you know you have "done" something? Where is the line between what is called "cooked" and what is merely assembled? You can't just heat up a peach and call it cooking, right? But you can heat it with a little wine and sugar, and now it's poached or baked.

After indulging in this philosophical tizzy for some time, what remains is this sandwich. It tastes delicious and, no doubt about it, the result is far greater than the sum of its parts. And if you've never thought of assembling these ingredients in this fashion and the outcome pleases you, then it pleases me as well. And that is what cooking is all about.

Egg Salad Sandwich

Makes about 3 sandwiches

I'm wild about eggs and always have been. Recently I learned that May is National Egg Month, and since that is my birth month, perhaps the egg and I were destined to have a close relationship.

There was a time when eggs were considered good thanks to their low calories and high protein. Then they were considered bad due to high cholesterol. Now they are back in nutritional favor, and I still love them.

If you don't want to use mustard, add some white vinegar for a little tang. And if you aren't going to serve the sandwich for a while, leave the walnuts out until it's time for assembly; otherwise, they become soggy.

4 large eggs

6 tablespoons Creamy Tofu Dressing (page 137), 3 for the egg salad and 3 for the bread

3 tablespoons toasted walnuts, coarsely chopped

1/2 teaspoon Dijon-style mustard or white vinegar

1/4 teaspoon salt

Freshly ground black pepper

Bread

Thinly sliced red onions

Lettuce

Place the eggs in a pan of cold water over high heat and bring to a boil. Turn off heat and cover. Let the eggs sit in the water for 20 minutes.

Remove the shells, mash the eggs with a fork, and add dressing, walnuts, mustard, salt, and pepper. Mix well and adjust for seasoning. Spread additional tofu dressing on the bread, and make sandwiches with the salad, onions, and lettuce.

Open-faced Smoked Salmon Sandwich

Makes 1 sandwich

In Mendocino, because we have access to quantities of locally caught salmon, we feel compelled to come up with new ways to deal with said fish. I love responsibilities like this, especially when I get to experiment with smoked salmon. This recipe was developed by Chris Kump. It is a very simple one, but the addition of the lemon juice is what turns it from pretty good to great.

We used to smoke our own salmon by soaking it in brine, drying it under a fan, and then putting it in a hot smoker along with wood chips. We used a Little Chief smoker that we bought at the discount store for about sixty dollars. It's a dynamite little unit and easy to use, if you wish to try smoking your own.

2 slices good-quality bread or 1 bagel, cut in half

About 4 tablespoons Herbed Cream Cheese (page 135)

2 to 3 ounces smoked salmon

A few drops freshly squeezed lemon juice

Freshly chopped dill

Freshly chopped parsley

Toast the bread or bagel. Spread Herbed Cream Cheese on both pieces. If the smoked salmon is dry, crumble it over the surfaces. If it is moist, slice the strips and lay them over the surface in a lattice design. Sprinkle with drops of lemon juice, then sprinkle with mixed herbs.

Smoked Turkey Salad Sandwich

Makes 4 or 5 sandwiches

Ideas for dishes often emerge from casual conversations. One season, a new sandwich was needed on the restaurant's menu, and with smoked turkey as the starting point, we created a hit that stayed for a few years. Take note, the quality of the smoked turkey is extremely important. Roundman's in Fort Bragg makes a delicious, top-quality product.

2/3 cup Mayonnaise (below)

2 1/2 tablespoons whole-grain mustard (I use Moutarde de Meaux)

1/2 cup currants, plumped in 1/2 cup tea for 15 minutes, then drained (I use Earl Grey)

1 pound smoked turkey, skinless, sliced very thin

Whole-wheat bread

1/3 cup slivered toasted almonds

About 1 1/2 cups young greens with a peppery flavor, such as arugula or watercress

1/2 cup Rhubarb Glop (page 14)

Mix together the mayonnaise, mustard, and currants, and fold in the turkey.

For each sandwich, place the turkey mixture on one slice of the bread, sprinkle with almonds, and place greens over the meat so they will peek out of the finished sandwich. Spread Glop on the other slice of bread and place on top.

Mayonnaise   Makes 2 1/2 cups

2 cups canola oil, or a mixture of olive and canola oils

1/4 cup vinegar (tarragon, rice, or sherry are good choices)

1/2 teaspoon salt

2 teaspoons Dijon-style mustard

1 whole egg and 3 egg yolks

In a food processor or blender, place 1/2 cup of the oil and all the other ingredients and blend for a few seconds to combine. With the motor running, pour in the remaining oil in a slow stream. The mixture will thicken by the time the last drop of oil is added or immediately thereafter.

Chicken Stock

Makes about 1 gallon

Baking chicken parts together with the vegetables before making a stock yields a deeper flavor than the more customary approach of using raw chicken parts and vegetables. Sometimes, this is the flavor difference I'm looking for. And don't be put off by what might seem to be a large yield. By the time you go to the trouble of making stock, for heaven's sake, make enough to have it be worth the time spent. Remember, you can always freeze the stock, and it's a handy ingredient to have around. Store-bought stock never tastes as good.

$6^{1}/_{2}$ pounds chicken necks and backs

3 yellow onions, peeled, and coarsely chopped

4 carrots, peeled, and cut into 1-inch pieces

4 stalks celery, cut into 1-inch pieces

2 bay leaves

2 teaspoons salt

5 cloves garlic, peeled

2 cups loosely packed parsley

Preheat the oven to 425°F.

Wash the chicken parts under cold water and dry with paper towels. Divide the parts into two portions and distribute between two shallow 10- by 15-inch roasting pans. Distribute the vegetables around chicken and place the pans in the oven. Bake for 1 hour, stirring every 15 minutes to coat the vegetables with pan juices.

Transfer the contents of the pans to a large pot, add 6 quarts cold water and the remainder of the ingredients. Bring to a boil and skim the surface foam, which will continue to appear for about 15 minutes.

Cover partially so that steam can escape, and simmer for about $1^{1}/_{2}$ hours.

Pour through a strainer and remove the fat with a large spoon. Refrigerate for several hours. Remove when the remaining fat has congealed and remove it.

Grandma Kump's Asparagus, Tarragon & Garlic Soup

Makes about 2 quarts

While my former husband and Beaujolais dinner chef, Chris Kump, specialized in fancy cooking, he also had what I called his "Grandma Kump" persona, in which he created more basic, simple, homey recipes, of which this is one. The rich flavor belies the low calories; no cream or butter is needed.

During the months that asparagus was in season, it found its way into many dishes on the Beaujolais menu. The more attractive tips were used in salads or as garnish and the stems wound up in soups. This actually could be retitled Name Your Own Vegetable Soup. Instead of asparagus, try spinach, broccoli, or cauliflower.

$3/4$ cup dry white vermouth

$1^1/2$ cups Chicken Stock (opposite)

3 cups water

1 pound yellow onions, coarsely chopped

1 to 4 cloves garlic, coarsely chopped

$1/4$ cup olive oil

2 pounds fresh asparagus (snap off the fibrous white ends and cut into 1-inch pieces)

Salt

White pepper

2 tablespoons fresh tarragon, minced

Place the vermouth, stock, and water in a large pot and bring to a boil. In a large skillet, sauté the onions and garlic in olive oil until soft, about 4 to 5 minutes. Add the asparagus and season well with salt and pepper.

Stirring constantly, continue to sauté over medium-high heat for 5 minutes, or until the asparagus is bright green and beginning to soften. Do not allow the onions and garlic to brown.

Empty the asparagus mixture into the pot containing the boiling stock, cover, and return to a boil over high heat, stirring occasionally. Continue boiling for 5 to 10 minutes, uncovered, just until the asparagus is softened. If you overcook it, the asparagus will lose its fresh, bright green color and turn quite drab and unappealing.

Remove from the heat, purée, pour through a sieve, and add the tarragon, salt, and pepper to taste. (If you don't care about calories, blend in up to $3/4$ cup of cream, or garnish with a dollop of lightly salted whipped cream or sour cream.)

Posole

Makes enough for 8 to 10 servings

Posole is a traditional Mexican dish that has many variations. I make no claim for authenticity as this recipe evolved over time and was influenced by a variety of other posole recipes as well as personal preferences. The flavors improve overnight, so make it a day ahead.

$2^1/2$ pounds country-style pork ribs, cut into 1-inch cubes

4 cups water

6 cups Chicken Stock (page 110)

$1^1/2$ cups beer

2 cups sliced onions

2 carrots, cut into 1-inch pieces

2 bay leaves

6 cloves garlic, coarsely chopped

1 tablespoon salt

1 teaspoon dried marjoram

2 (15-ounce) cans white hominy, drained

3 dried pasilla peppers

Place all ingredients, except for the hominy and pasilla peppers, in a large pot, cover, and bring to a boil. Reduce heat and cook over medium heat for about 1 to $1^1/2$ hours until pork is tender.

Refrigerate for at least 6 hours, then degrease thoroughly. Taste for salt and adjust as needed. Add hominy.

Toast the pasillas in a dry frying pan over medium heat until fragrant, a few minutes, stirring to prevent burning.

Transfer to a bowl of hot water, enough to cover the pasillas, for 10 minutes, then drain, purée, and pass through a strainer. Add puréed chiles to the soup and stir well to combine.

To serve, assemble the following and place on the table for each diner to add to the soup: quartered limes, chopped cilantro, minced green onions, finely shredded green cabbage, sliced radishes, and sliced avocado.

Spinach & Mint Soup

Makes 1 serving

My mom makes a delicious spinach and mint salad, and it occurred to me that it could be turned into an excellent soup. It's not going to change your life, but the flavors have a nice zing, without demanding that your taste buds accept something dramatically offbeat.

It is important to use only the leaves of the spinach, so be sure to remove the stems. Of course, the leaves must be washed thoroughly to remove the sand and grit.

1 cup Chicken Stock (page 110)

1 cup fresh spinach, ribbed and cleaned

1 to 2 teaspoons chopped fresh mint

A few drops lemon juice

2 tablespoons cubed tofu

2 to 3 tablespoons cooked garbanzo beans

Salt

Pepper

1 slice lemon

Bring the chicken stock to a boil. Reduce the heat slightly and add the spinach. Cook for about 30 seconds, then add the rest of the ingredients, except for the lemon slice, seasoning to taste. After 30 seconds, pour into a bowl, and garnish with the lemon slice.

Roasted Butternut Squash Soup

Makes 6 servings

A few times a year I used to teach weekend cooking classes at Linda Reuther's Hearts & Hands, a relaxing and restorative retreat center in Albion, about 10 miles south of Mendocino. In the old-fashioned kitchen of the antiques-filled 1860s farmhouse, several students prepare a seasonal menu that we all enjoy for dinner. The next morning, after a stroll around the apple orchard, meadows, and along Cider Creek, we sit down for a hearty Beaujolais-style breakfast for the students and the staff. This soup was created for a fall class and shows off the ingredients that are available throughout the winter.

About 2$1/2$ to 3 pounds butternut squash

$1/3$ cup unsalted butter

2$1/2$ cups chopped onions

6 cups Gingered Vegetable Broth (page 116) or Chicken Stock (page 110)

Salt

Freshly ground pepper

Freshly grated nutmeg

1$1/4$ cups peeled and finely chopped apple

8 fresh sage leaves, chopped

Preheat the oven to 400°F.

Prick the squash with the tip of a knife so it won't explode during baking. Place on a baking sheet and roast until soft to the touch, about 1 hour. A knife should penetrate the skin easily. Remove from the oven and let cool.

Cut in half lengthwise and remove and discard seeds and fibers. Scoop out the pulp into a bowl and set aside.

In a saucepan over low heat, melt all but 1 tablespoon of butter and add the onions, stirring occasionally, until the onions are tender, 8 to 10 minutes. Add the broth and the squash pulp, raise the heat to high, and bring to a boil. Reduce heat to low and simmer for 10 minutes. Remove from heat.

Purée the soup in a blender or food processor. Return the purée to a clean saucepan. Reheat, gently, over medium heat and season with salt, pepper, and nutmeg, as needed.

While you are doing this, heat the remaining butter in a small pan over medium heat. Add the apple and cook for about 3 minutes, until soft but not mushy. Season with nutmeg and set aside.

To serve, ladle soup into warmed bowls. Distribute the sautéed apples evenly among the bowls and garnish with sage leaves.

CONTINUED

Roasted Butternut Squash Soup

Gingered Vegetable Broth—the quick way

3 carrots, coarsely chopped

1 onion, coarsely chopped

3 stalks celery, coarsely chopped

1 cup parsley, coarsely chopped

6 cloves garlic, coarsely chopped

1 fragrant bay leaf

$3/4$ cup peeled and chopped fresh ginger

6 sprigs fresh thyme

$8^1/2$ cups water

$1^3/4$ teaspoons salt

Freshly ground pepper

Place all ingredients in a saucepan, cover, and bring to a boil. Remove cover and let simmer for 30 minutes. Strain and discard vegetables.

No Magic Potion Needed

Great cooking isn't magic. It is *not* about exotic ingredients, professional-grade equipment, and flashy techniques. In the classes I've been teaching over the past thirty-five years, I encourage my students to build a repertoire of basic favorites they can return to over and over again. Although today's popular cooking shows and gourmet magazines often partner complex combinations with stylish but hard-to-master execution, the dishes that will be most useful in your daily life are the tried-and-true standbys. I don't mean boring—no, no, no! I do mean that whatever you make should not involve a three-ring-circus of endless preparation and painstaking presentation. Keep it simple to start with and you'll be encouraged to continue. After all, nothing builds confidence like success.

Cold Fusion Soup

Makes 6 servings

At a private tasting of Charles B. Mitchell wines hosted by Jill Mitchell, former chef for her family's winery in Fair Play, California, I was especially dazzled by the lovely, soft Riesling. I asked if she had considered how well it would complement fruit desserts. One step ahead of me, Jill said she had already created an unusual dessert to emphasize the wine's mango, quince, and honey undertones.

Soup Base

24 ounces (by weight) frozen mango chunks (available in many supermarkets) or the equivalent in fresh fruit, peeled, seeded, and weighed

1 1/3 cups Riesling wine (a favorite of mine is from the Charles B. Mitchell Winery)

Topping

1 cup heavy whipping cream

1 tablespoon sugar

1/2 teaspoon almond extract

1/8 teaspoon ground coriander

1/2 teaspoon ground cardamom

1/2 teaspoon finely grated Meyer lemon zest

2 teaspoons Meyer lemon juice

Garnish

1/2 cup raspberries

Mint sprigs

For the soup base: Place the mango and the Riesling in a blender and purée.

For the topping: Place all the topping ingredients in a medium-sized bowl and beat until soft peaks form.

Pour soup into small, chilled serving bowls or sturdy wine goblets. Place a few berries in the center of the soup surface and add a big dollop of topping onto the berry base. Top with a mint sprig and serve with a well-chilled glass of the same Riesling used in the soup.

SIDE DISHES & SALADS

Kasspatzl
120

Creamy Polenta
121

Crunchy Country Fries
122

Savory Country Fries
123

Crunchy Country Fries
Extravaganza
124

Chris's Waldorf Salad
126

Margaret's Walking Salad
127

Red & Green Coleslaw with
Orange Dressing
128

Citrus Salad
129

Pamela Imbach's Famous
French Potato Salad
130

Pasta Salad
131

Kasspatzl

Makes 6 servings as a side dish

Another Austrian tribute to noodles and dumplings—just a few ingredients that produce a dish to go with a salad on the side or a satisfying accompaniment to a meat or chicken dish with sauce. A search on the Internet revealed that spatzle makers are readily available and quite inexpensive. My Austrian friend, Andrea Gritsch, let me hover by her side, American measuring utensils in hand, while she demonstrated how to make this dish "spatzle-ty." (Note to gastro-etymologists: In the local dialect, there is no umlaut over the "a" in spatzle.)

2 3/4 cups white flour

3/4 teaspoon salt

2 large eggs

1/3 cup milk

About 3/4 cup cold water

1 1/2 cups finely chopped yellow onions

1/4 cup unsalted butter

6 ounces cheese: grated, full-flavored Swiss, or finely cut-up Gorgonzola, or a combination of the two

1/2 cup smoked ham cut into 1/4-inch cubes (optional)

About 2 tablespoons finely chopped chives

In a large pot, bring 3 quarts of water to a boil. Add 2 tablespoons salt.

In a medium-sized bowl, combine flour and 3/4 teaspoon salt. Add the eggs and milk and, while whisking, gradually add up to 3/4 cup water, stirring just enough to combine. The dough will be wet and elastic.

Place a spatzle maker over the boiling water, fill, and push back and forth quickly until all the batter is used up. Stir noodles briefly while bringing the water to a boil again. Cook while gently boiling for no more than 5 minutes. Strain, rinse thoroughly in cold water, and let drain.

Slowly sauté onions in butter over low to medium heat until richly browned, about 15 minutes or more. Stir into the spatzle, along with the optional cheese and ham, and mix thoroughly.

Turn into a buttered 5-cup-capacity baking dish and bake at 350°F for 10 minutes, or until heated through and bubbling around the edges. Sprinkle with chives and serve.

Creamy Polenta

Makes 4 to 5 servings

Roberta Wright, former cook at Cafe Beaujolais, used to amaze me with her ability to create dishes both simple and intricate. At one end of the spectrum, she was a fantastic baker whose creations made our customers gasp. And at the other end, she came up with homey preparations that were also scrumptious. This creamy polenta is one of the latter.

5 cups liquid: at least 3, but up to 5 of milk; 2 or fewer of water or Chicken Stock (page 110)

3/4 teaspoon salt

1/4 teaspoon Tabasco sauce (omit if your topping is sweet)

1 cup dry polenta

Topping of your choice

In a heavy-bottomed saucepan, bring the liquid to a simmer. Add the salt and Tabasco sauce, pour the polenta into the liquid in a heavy stream, whisking constantly, over medium heat for about 12 to 15 minutes.

Pour into warm bowls and add the topping of your choice.

Sweet Toppings

Maple syrup or brown sugar and milk: These are the simplest, and most comforting, toppings for a simple and comforting breakfast. Think of it as the morning-food equivalent of chicken soup. Come to think of it, I *have* eaten Creamy Polenta with either a little maple syrup or brown sugar and milk in the evening when I've been ill, just as I've eaten chicken soup for breakfast. It all goes to show....

Savory Toppings

Mexican topping: Sprinkle polenta with 2 tablespoons cheese, then drizzle 2 tablespoons warmed salsa over the top. Garnish with chopped cilantro. You may wish to add a few tablespoons of Black Bean Chili (page 153) to a bed of polenta, and follow with Mexican topping.

Italian topping: Swirl 1 or 2 teaspoons Pesto (page 141) into the polenta, and sprinkle grated Parmesan cheese on top. Place in a hot oven for 1 minute to melt. For a more substantial dish, consider adding some spicy Italian sausage links, cut into chunks, and/or some Tomato-Eggplant Sauce (page 136).

Almost anything else under the sun: The taste of polenta is sufficiently mild that virtually any topping you can think of, from beef gravy to Rhubarb Glop, will probably be just fine.

Wait—just kidding about the Rhubarb Glop.

Crunchy Country Fries

Makes 1 to 2 servings

Our customers loved our fried potatoes and always asked, "What do you *do* to them?" The fact is, we didn't really do much of anything except boil red potatoes, cool them, slice them, and fry them in butter and oil on the grill. That's it. No seasonings, no nothing. The only things you have to remember, and this is important, is to boil them in salted water just until done, wait to sauté them until they are totally chilled all the way through, and sauté them long enough to get really crispy.

Use a cast-iron skillet, if available. The sticking that a nonstick pan avoids is the very thing you want to encourage. It's what helps the crunchy crispiness to develop. That, and taking your time. Don't be in a hurry.

3/4 pound small red potatoes, unpeeled

1 tablespoon salt

2 tablespoons butter, olive oil, canola oil, or a mixture

1 tablespoon sour cream

Place the potatoes in a medium-sized saucepan, cover with 1 quart cold water, and add salt. Cover and bring to a boil, then reduce heat and cook until just tender. Do not let potatoes get overdone.

Drain, rinse in cold water, drain again, and refrigerate until cold, several hours or overnight. Cut into 3/4-inch cubes or slice thinly, about 1/8 inch.

Heat the butter/oil in a 10-inch skillet, and when the pan is hot, add the potatoes. Sauté for about 10 minutes over medium-high heat, flipping the potatoes when brown. Continue to cook to develop crispiness on all sides. When done, transfer to a warm plate and garnish with sour cream.

Savory Country Fries

Makes 2 to 3 servings

3/4 pound small red potatoes, boiled and chilled, for Crunchy Country Fries (opposite)

2 to 3 tablespoons butter, olive oil, canola oil, or a mixture

1 cup minced red onions

1 teaspoon minced garlic

1 tablespoon sour cream

1 tablespoon finely chopped parsley

Freshly ground black pepper

Heat 1 tablespoon butter/oil in a 10-inch skillet. When the pan is hot, add the onions, turn heat to medium-low, and sauté until soft but not brown, stirring frequently, about 10 minutes. Add garlic and continue cooking over a low heat for an additional 2 minutes. The garlic wants to burn, so stir frequently. Transfer to a bowl.

Cut the potatoes into 3/4-inch cubes or slice thinly, about 1/8 inch. Heat the skillet, add 2 tablespoons butter/oil, and add potatoes. Sauté for about 10 minutes, until brown and crispy. Add onion and garlic mixture, cook for another 2 minutes, or until heated through. Transfer to a warm plate and garnish with sour cream, parsley, and pepper.

Add any or all of the following at the specified times:

Grated cheese, about 30 seconds before cooking is completed

Cooked vegetable(s) of your choice (I like broccoli), about 2 minutes before cooking is completed to heat through

Caraway seeds, a pinch or two when the potatoes are halfway done

Salsa, along with the sour cream

Crunchy Country Fries Extravaganza

Makes 2 servings

This was the kind of attention-getting dish that made new arrivals ask, "*What* are those people in the corner eating?"

Crunchy Country Fries (page 122)

1 tablespoon butter, olive oil, canola oil, or a mixture

1 teaspoon minced garlic

1 teaspoon Beaujolais Blend Herbs* or dried oregano

2/3 cup sliced mushrooms

1/3 cup finely chopped green onions

1/3 cup grated Jack or Cheddar cheese

Sour cream

* Beaujolais Blend Herbs are available from Fuller's Fine Herbs (www.fullersfineherbs.com)

While you are preparing the fries, heat a separate pan and add the butter. When melted, add the garlic and herbs. Stir over medium-low heat for about 30 seconds without letting the garlic brown, and add the mushrooms. Turn heat up and sauté until the mushrooms are cooked through. Drain and reserve liquid for another use, such as soup.

Add the green onions to the potatoes about 2 minutes before potatoes are done, and cook until the onions are soft. Add the mushrooms and grated cheese and cover the pan to melt the cheese. Stir, then transfer to a heated plate and garnish with sour cream. After eating, take a nap.

Chris's Waldorf Salad

Makes 4 to 5 servings

Those with childhood memories of Waldorf salad will find this a more sophisticated rendition. Just be sure to prepare shortly before serving, or the apples will turn brown.

4 crisp apples

2 tablespoons lime juice

$1/3$ cup currants

$1/2$ cup thinly sliced celery

$2/3$ cup Orange-Lime Mayonnaise (below)

$2/3$ cup coarsely chopped toasted walnuts

Core the apples, and cube them, about $3/8$ inch. Toss with the lime juice.

Add the currants, celery, and mayonnaise and mix to coat evenly. Add walnuts just before serving.

Orange-Lime Mayonnaise

1 cup canola oil

Finely grated zest of 1 orange

Finely grated zest of 1 lime

1 tablespoon orange juice, strained

1 tablespoon lime juice, strained

1 teaspoon Dijon-style mustard

$1/4$ teaspoon salt

2 egg yolks

In a food processor, place $1/4$ cup oil and the rest of the ingredients, and blend. With the motor running, add the remaining oil very slowly. The mayonnaise will thicken by the time all the oil is added.

Margaret's Walking Salad

This is a recipe from my Girl Scout days (Troop 2183, El Cerrito, California) that I've gussied up a bit. Who says you can't go home again? You simply take a different route.

Mix a little finely grated orange zest into sweetened cream cheese, ricotta, whipped cottage cheese, or yogurt cheese, spread on an apple half, and dot with raisins and a few chopped toasted walnuts. Eat on the go.

And They Kill It Humanely, Too

Did you know that salt added after a dish is cooked never functions as well as salt added during the cooking? It's best from the inside out, so to speak, because it flavors the food completely. Years ago, after an impromptu salt tasting with my friend Barbara Tropp, I switched from plain salt to kosher salt. We tasted different salt varieties: plain, kosher, sea. I couldn't believe the difference. She, a devout believer in kosher, converted me in an instant. The kosher tasted pure and unadulterated. However, it takes about twice the volume of the kosher salt to equal the same amount of other kinds (it is much lighter in weight), and I could never get the restaurant staff used to changing recipes with that in mind. Eventually, the kitchen switched to sea salt. Nowadays, different brands of sea salts from around the world abound.

Red & Green Coleslaw with Orange Dressing

Makes 6 to 8 servings

When I first published this recipe in the late 1980s, I had to explain what a jicama was, how you pronounce it, along with a little pep talk on being assertive when you can't find one in the market, because it should be there. Surely, I don't have to do this anymore, do I?

Freshly grated zest of 1 orange

1/4 cup freshly squeezed orange juice

1 tablespoon freshly squeezed lemon juice

1/3 cup olive oil

Salt

Freshly ground black pepper

1/4 head each red and green cabbage, finely shredded

1/4 jicama, peeled, and cut into matchsticks

2 tablespoons poppy seeds

2 oranges, peeled, and segmented (see Citrus Salad, opposite, for technique)

Mix together the zest, juices, oil, salt, and pepper.

In a separate bowl, combine the cabbage and jicama. Add the poppy seeds and dressing. Toss and adjust for salt and pepper. Gently add the orange segments and serve.

Citrus Salad

Makes 6 servings

This salad is from my youth, when my mom often made inventive salads. I thought it was the height of sophistication because of the grapefruit. Go figure.

Neatness counts in the preparation. The segments must be pristine. If the orange and grapefruit segments are less than perfectly sliced, the dish looks like a mess. Which takes me back to an experience from the early 1980s. I was on staff at the Great Chefs of France Cooking School at the Mondavi Winery, and that session's culinary master was Michel Guérard, a three-star chef. You don't acquire three stars by accident. It comes from years and years of training and hard, dedicated work, and that's just the beginning. The chef asked me to segment an entire case of grapefruit (48), first removing every bit of white pith, *s'il vous plait*. When I proudly returned with my denuded case, he took one look and sent me right back to the kitchen to do it properly. My version of perfect wasn't perfect enough for him. That was a humbling experience. A very sharp knife makes the job much easier.

1 head young romaine lettuce

¹/₂ cup light olive oil

2 tablespoons sherry vinegar or Japanese rice vinegar

Salt

Freshly ground black pepper

1 teaspoon minced garlic

1 teaspoon Dijon-style prepared mustard

1 teaspoon minced fresh tarragon

1 small red onion, sliced very thinly

1 grapefruit

1 orange

1 avocado

Wash and dry the lettuce leaves thoroughly and place in the refrigerator.

Prepare the vinaigrette by mixing together the oil, vinegar, salt, pepper, garlic, mustard, and tarragon. Add the sliced onion and marinate for up to 4 hours.

With a very sharp knife, remove the entire peel and the pith from the grapefruit and orange. (Until you are adept at this, you *will* waste some of the fruit. Sorry.) Hold the peeled grapefruit in your hand; the segments should be apparent. Remove the individual wedges by cutting toward the center on both sides of each membrane. The wedges should come out fairly easily, and intact. Repeat the procedure with the orange.

When ready to serve the salad, peel the avocado and slice it. Toss the lettuce with the vinaigrette, reserving the onions. Gently toss with the segments, garnish with avocado slices and marinated onion rings.

Pamela Imbach's Famous French Potato Salad

Makes 6 servings

After a few days of recipe-testing at my parents' house, my mom's eyes glazed over as she announced, "You must be reacting to your childhood experiences of potato deprivation." She 'fessed up to having often made one lone potato suffice for our entire family due to a mistaken belief that potatoes were fattening. To compensate, I used to play with Mr. Potato Head a lot. Now, I can work with the real thing, and I'm making up for lost time.

Pam Imbach is a fabulous Napa Valley cook who introduced me to using vinaigrette instead of mayonnaise in potato salad.

$2^{1}/_{2}$ pounds red potatoes (similar in size), unpeeled

1 teaspoon salt

Freshly ground black pepper

2 tablespoons Dijon-style mustard

3 tablespoons red wine vinegar

1 teaspoon minced garlic

$^{1}/_{2}$ cup olive oil

$^{3}/_{4}$ cup finely chopped green onions

$^{3}/_{4}$ cup minced parsley

3 hard-boiled eggs, chopped (optional)

Place the potatoes in a large pot, cover with cold water, and add salt (1 tablespoon for every quart water). Cover and bring to a boil, turn heat to medium, and continue cooking for 10 to 20 minutes, until tender when pierced with a fork.

Remove from heat, drain, and let sit for 15 minutes, until warm.

Meanwhile, combine all the other ingredients except for the eggs.

Cut the warm potatoes into $^{3}/_{4}$-inch cubes, place in a large bowl, and add the dressing. Mix with care; rough handling will result in mashed potato salad. Adjust for seasoning. Mix again every half hour. When ready to serve, taste again for seasoning. If refrigerated, the potatoes may require more salt and pepper. Add the eggs, if desired, just before serving.

Pasta Salad

Makes 6 to 8 servings

The sky is the limit on additions, subtractions, and variations. Depending on how much of your meal you want this pasta salad to occupy, you can keep it fairly simple, or amplify it by adding crumbled feta cheese, tomatoes, and Greek olives—the really tasty ones; not the bland ones you stick on your fingers and wave around at parties. Serve it on a bed of lettuce and you have an entrée.

Most important, cook the pasta properly—no dumping it in boiling salted water and walking away. Test it often, and drain when it is neither too hard nor too soft.

The salad can be refrigerated, but I think it is even better at room temperature, never having been chilled. Alternatively, there is no reason why it can't be served warm. Preheat all the ingredients, except the cheese, then mix everything including the cheese together and serve in warm bowls.

1 pound dried pasta, any shape other than long and flat (my favorite is the corkscrew-shaped fusilli)

2/3 cup olive oil

Salt

Pepper

1 tablespoon lemon juice

2 tablespoons balsamic or sherry vinegar

1 teaspoon minced garlic

2 tablespoons finely chopped fresh basil

Finely grated zest of 1 lemon

1/2 cup finely chopped green onions

1/3 cup toasted pine nuts

1/2 cup grated dry cheese (Asiago, dry Monterey Jack, or Parmesan)

3 tablespoons minced chives

1/2 cup finely diced red bell peppers

Cook the pasta in boiling water until just tender, but not at all mushy, about 8 to 10 minutes. Drain and transfer to a large bowl. Mix together the oil, salt and pepper, lemon juice, vinegar, garlic, basil, and lemon zest in a separate container, then toss with the pasta. Let cool, add the remaining ingredients, and adjust seasoning.

SpreAds, sAuces & DressINgs

Dried Tomato Spread
134

Cranberry Sauce
134

Crème Fraîche
135

Herbed Cream Cheese
135

Nut Oil Mayonnaise
136

Tomato-Eggplant Sauce
136

Creamy Tofu Dressing
137

Smoked Turkey Pasta Sauce
138

Goat Cheese Pasta Sauce
139

Spicy Sausage Sauce
140

Pesto
141

Salsa
141

Pico de Gallo Relish
142

Multi-purpose Apricot Sauce
143

A Bunch of Salad Dressings
144

Dried Tomato Spread

Makes about ¹/₂ cup

This spread is extremely versatile and will keep for several months, covered, in the refrigerator. I use it in soup, in salads, mixed into scrambled eggs while they're cooking, as an omelette filling, in biscuit dough, as a garnish on a homemade pizza, and as a sandwich spread. Be sure to use a small saucepan. Mine was too big the first time around, and I ended up with crackly blackened tomatoes on the bottom.

1 cup (about 1 ounce) dried sliced tomatoes
¹/₂ cup water
2 teaspoons minced garlic
¹/₄ cup olive oil

In a small pot, place tomatoes, water, garlic, and 2 tablespoons of the oil. Bring to a boil and cover, then reduce heat to very low. Simmer gently for about 1 hour, until the tomatoes are extremely soft. Check frequently to make sure that the liquid has not evaporated. (If it does evaporate, add up to 3 tablespoons of water; but if the tomatoes are already burnt, you can only throw them away.) Add the remaining 2 tablespoons of olive oil. Either purée in a food processor to make a paste, or leave the tomato slices whole. Let cool completely, then cover and refrigerate.

Cranberry Sauce

Makes about 2¹/₄ cups

I don't like tart things when they are made too sweet, so I tend to keep them pretty tart. If you prefer your cranberry sauce sweeter, use the full cup of white sugar, or even a bit more. The wine adds a depth of flavor not found in commercial brands of sauce.

I wish fresh cranberries were available all year round. When they are in season, in late fall, I buy huge quantities and freeze them for use throughout the year.

³/₄ to 1 cup white sugar
1 cup red wine
¹/₂ cinnamon stick
3 cups fresh or frozen cranberries
Grated zest of 1 orange

In a saucepan, combine the sugar, wine, and cinnamon stick. Bring to a boil, stirring occasionally. Reduce the heat and boil gently for 3 minutes.

Discard any unsatisfactory looking cranberries and rinse the good ones. Add the cranberries and grated orange zest and simmer for 10 minutes. Remove from the heat and let cool. Remove the cinnamon stick.

Crème Fraîche

Makes as much as you want

Crème fraîche has a multitude of uses: as a topping for fruit, whipped into soups, or stirred into sauces. It doesn't break down when it's heated the way sour cream and yogurt do. It also has a mellower flavor—nutty, instead of tangy.

Heavy whipping cream (as many cups as you wish)

Buttermilk (1 tablespoon per each cup of cream)

Combine the cream and buttermilk in a saucepan over medium heat. Heat just until the chill is off—to about 90°F. Pour into a glass jar, cover lightly with a piece of waxed paper, and let sit in a warm place, 65°F to 70°F, for 12 to 20 hours, until it has thickened.

Replace the waxed paper with plastic wrap or a tight-fitting lid, and refrigerate for at least 6 hours before using. Keeps up to 2 weeks.

Herbed Cream Cheese

Makes about 2¹/₂ pounds

This is an all-purpose spread and/or dip. You can substitute goat cheese in place of, or in addition to, the natural cream cheese.

1 tablespoon chopped chives

3 tablespoons chopped parsley

4 tablespoons chopped green onions (white and green sections)

1 tablespoon, plus 2 teaspoons chopped garlic

1¹/₂ tablespoons vinegar (I prefer tarragon vinegar)

¹/₄ teaspoon freshly and finely ground black pepper

2¹/₂ pounds natural cream cheese, fresh goat cheese, or a combination of the two

Place all the ingredients, except the cheese, in a food processor and process for 15 seconds. Place the cheese in the bowl of an electric mixer, add the herb mixture, and beat thoroughly. The finished product keeps about a week in the refrigerator.

A tablespoon of the herb mixture alone (no cream cheese) can be added to ¹/₂ cup mayonnaise for use on sandwiches or hamburgers.

Nut Oil Mayonnaise

Makes about 1¹/4 cups

This variation on basic mayonnaise is an especially good accompaniment to cold artichokes.

³/4 cup canola oil

2 tablespoons white wine vinegar

¹/4 teaspoon salt

1 teaspoon Dijon mustard

2 egg yolks

¹/4 cup walnut or hazelnut oil

¹/4 cup toasted walnuts or hazelnuts, chopped

In a food processor or blender, place ¹/4 cup of the canola oil and all the other ingredients, except for the nut oil and the nuts, and blend. With the motor running, slowly add the remaining canola oil and nut oil in a thin stream. The mayonnaise will thicken by the time the last drop of oil is added. When you are ready to use the mayonnaise, stir in the nuts and proceed with your recipe.

Tomato-Eggplant Sauce

Makes about 1 quart

This wonderful sauce must be credited to Marcella Hazan; if it isn't exactly hers, it is very, very close. The main difference is that I bake the eggplant instead of sautéeing it. Be very sure the eggplant is well cooked. There is nothing even remotely worthwhile about crunchy eggplant.

1 pound eggplant, diced into 2-inch pieces

¹/4 cup olive oil

2 teaspoons minced garlic

¹/4 cup finely chopped parsley

2 cups canned tomatoes (I use Muir Glen Organic)

¹/2 teaspoon red pepper flakes

Salt

Freshly ground black pepper

Preheat the oven to 375°F.

In a bowl, mix together eggplant and olive oil. Spread out in a thin layer on a 10- by 15-inch baking sheet.

Bake until the eggplant is soft and fully cooked, about 1 hour. Stir frequently, especially during the last half of the baking time.

Pour off the oil into a heavy-bottomed pot and cook the garlic in it over low heat for about 3 minutes, stirring frequently. Add the parsley, tomatoes, and red pepper flakes, and cook for 25 minutes. Stir in the eggplant and simmer for 5 minutes more. Taste for seasoning.

Creamy Tofu Dressing

Makes about 1¹/₄ cups

Use this as a salad dressing, a dip, a baked potato topping, or a mayonnaise substitute.

2 tablespoons lemon juice

2 tablespoons canola oil

2 teaspoons soy sauce

¹/₄ teaspoon salt

2 tablespoons chopped yellow onions

¹/₄ cup green onions, finely chopped

1¹/₂ teaspoons minced garlic

3 tablespoons packed chopped parsley

¹/₄ teaspoon curry powder

8 ounces firm tofu, rinsed, drained, and dried with a paper towel

Place all ingredients, except the tofu, in a blender or food processor, and blend thoroughly. Add the tofu and blend until smooth.

Refrigerate overnight to give flavors a chance to meld. Lasts up to 5 days.

Smoked Turkey Pasta Sauce

Makes enough for 2 servings of pasta

This recipe is very rich in flavor—and cream—which you may wish to decrease by adding some pasta cooking liquid (try 2 tablespoons to begin) to the white wine after reducing it, and decreasing the cream by the same amount.

1 cup dry white wine

1 tablespoon finely chopped shallots

1/4 cup finely diced carrots

2 tablespoons finely sliced celery

2 teaspoons whole-grain or Dijon-style mustard

1/2 cup heavy whipping cream

1/8 teaspoon freshly grated nutmeg

2 cups thinly ribboned spinach, or greens of your choice

5 ounces slivered strips (not slices) smoked turkey

Salt

Freshly ground black pepper

Hot cooked pasta

Place the wine, shallots, carrots, and celery into a small saucepan, bring to a boil. Turn heat to medium and reduce by half, about 10 minutes. The vegetables should be tender before you proceed. Add the mustard, cream, and nutmeg, and continue cooking for about 2 minutes more, until slightly thickened, while stirring occasionally. Add the spinach and turkey, and cook for about 1 minute or so, until the spinach is tender and the meat heated through.

Taste for seasoning and pour over hot pasta. Stir gently to combine.

Goat Cheese Pasta Sauce

Makes enough for 4 servings of pasta

But then, who knows what "pasta for 4" means? This subject once precipitated a near brawl at the restaurant. I'd suggest starting with 3 ounces (dry weight) per person to see how it goes. Be careful not to cook the sauce after mixing it with the pasta, or the ingredients will separate and the dish will look very unappetizing.

Hot cooked pasta

$1/4$ cup pine nuts

6 ounces goat cheese

$1/3$ to $1/2$ cup reserved pasta cooking water

3 tablespoons olive oil

2 teaspoons minced garlic

Freshly ground black pepper

$1/2$ cup finely chopped green onions

6 strips crisp bacon, crumbled

2 ounces grated dry cheese

About 16 cherry tomatoes, cut in half

1 tablespoon chopped fresh basil

Toast pine nuts in a 325°F oven for about 10 minutes, until golden brown. Remove and cool.

Mix together goat cheese, reserved pasta cooking water, olive oil, garlic, and pepper until smooth.

Transfer pasta to a large warmed bowl and add all the ingredients, except the basil. Mix to combine, divide among 4 warmed bowls, garnish with basil, and serve.

Spicy Sausage Sauce

Makes enough for 4 servings

For this rich combination of sausage and cream, high-quality sausage is essential. Here on the north coast in Fort Bragg, just north of Mendocino, we are lucky to have family owned Roundman's Smoke House and Butcher Shop.

2 tablespoons olive oil

2 cups thinly sliced or chopped bell peppers

12 ounces sliced andouille or linguisa sausage

1/2 teaspoon crushed red pepper

1 teaspoon minced garlic

2 cups dry white wine

2/3 cup whipping cream

6 tablespoons chopped green onions

1/4 cup grated dry cheese (Parmesan, dry Asiago, or dry Jack)

1 pound hot cooked pasta, with about 1/2 cup of the cooking water retained separately

Minced parsley

In a large sauté pan, heat the oil and add the peppers, cooking over medium heat until limp. Add the sausage, red pepper, and garlic and cook until the sausage is lightly browned. Add the white wine, bring to a boil, lower the heat, and reduce the liquid by about a third. Add the cream and green onions and cook until slightly thickened. Combine with the dry cheese, pasta, and cooking water and serve, garnished with minced parsley.

Pesto

Makes 1¹/₄ cups

Pesto must be one of Italy's most magnificent culinary contributions. I like it in mayonnaise and salad dressings, on pasta, in soups, as a sandwich spread, and as an omelette filling. In fact, I've been known to invent recipes just to have more excuses to use pesto!

2 cups firmly packed fresh (it is a waste of ingredients to ever use dried) basil leaves (stalks and stems are okay, if using a food processor)

¹/₂ cup freshly grated dry cheese (Parmesan, dry Monterey Jack, or Asiago)

¹/₂ teaspoon salt

2 large cloves garlic

¹/₂ cup olive oil

¹/₄ cup pine nuts (optional)

In a food processor or blender, combine all the ingredients until smooth. Store for up to 1 week in refrigerator, or indefinitely in freezer.

Salsa

Makes about 2¹/₂ cups

Adjust the heat to your liking by adding as much or as little jalapeño as you wish.

2 medium ripe red tomatoes

2 tablespoons white wine vinegar

1 teaspoon minced garlic

1 teaspoon dried oregano (if using fresh, 2 teaspoons, minced)

¹/₂ to 1 teaspoon salt

¹/₃ cup minced red onions

¹/₄ cup finely chopped green onions

¹/₄ cup coarsely chopped cilantro

1 to 2 jalapeño chiles, seeded, stemmed, and minced

Core the tomatoes and chop. Combine with the rest of the ingredients.

Pico de Gallo Relish

Makes about 3 cups

Pico de Gallo means "beak of the rooster" and, of course, you are pronouncing it "GUY-oh" and not like the name of the folks who sell wine.

1/4 cup finely chopped red onions

2 oranges, peeled, and thinly sliced crosswise (save the juice)

4 to 5 ounces (1/2 to 2/3 cup) peeled cucumbers, cut in half lengthwise, large seeds removed, then sliced again into thin half moons

4 ounces (1 cup) peeled jicama, cut into matchsticks

Half of 1 red bell pepper, cut into matchsticks

2 ounces (1/2 to 2/3 cup) peeled carrot, sliced 1/16 inch (optional)

2 tablespoons olive oil

1 tablespoon white wine vinegar

1/2 teaspoon salt

Pinch of cayenne pepper

Pinch of chopped fresh oregano

1/2 teaspoon crushed red pepper flakes

1/4 cup fresh orange juice (use saved juice from above)

1 to 2 tablespoons lime juice (optional)

Mix together the onions, oranges, cucumbers, jicama, red peppers, and carrots (if desired) in a large bowl. Blend the remaining ingredients in a small bowl and pour over the vegetables. Mix together and adjust the seasoning.

Multi-purpose Apricot Sauce

Makes about 2 cups

I may not seem like an apricots-in-heavy-syrup kind of gal, but the sauce from said fruit can be partnered with some of my favorite foods: under cakes, over waffles, or with ice cream.

1 (15^1/$_2$-ounce) can apricots in heavy syrup

^{1}/$_4$ teaspoon freshly ground nutmeg

^{1}/$_4$ teaspoon cinnamon

^{1}/$_8$ teaspoon powdered cloves

3 tablespoons dark rum

^{1}/$_2$ teaspoon vanilla extract

1 teaspoon minced candied ginger (optional)

Place the apricots and syrup in a small pot, cover, and bring to a boil.

Reduce heat to low and simmer until very soft, about 15 minutes, stirring occasionally.

Pour into a blender or food processor, and add the remaining ingredients, except for the optional ginger. Blend until smooth, then add ginger.

A Bunch of Salad Dressings

Use a really good oil and vinegar for your dressings and your palate will thank you. If the salad includes nuts, use the oil of that nut in the recipe. However, nut oils can be extremely intense, so you will have to use part canola or light olive oil as well. If garlic is included, be sure to refrigerate the dressing to prevent botulism.

Basic Vinaigrette   Makes about 2¹/₂ cups

¹/₂ cup herb-flavored white wine vinegar or sherry vinegar

2 tablespoons Dijon-style prepared mustard

1 teaspoon minced garlic

1 teaspoon salt

Freshly ground black pepper

2 cups oil(s) of your choice

Mix all the ingredients together. Adjust seasoning. Shake before serving.

Herb-Flavored Vinegar

Place a bunch of the fresh herb of your choice in a clean jar. Tarragon or basil is especially good. Heat white wine vinegar and pour into the jar to cover the herb. Cover tightly and let stand in a cool, dark place for three weeks; strain the vinegar to remove the herb.

Hazelnut or Walnut Oil Dressing   Makes 1 cup

¹/₄ cup freshly squeezed lemon juice

¹/₂ cup hazelnut or walnut oil

¹/₄ cup canola oil

Salt

Freshly ground black pepper

Whisk all ingredients together until combined.

Goat Cheese Dressing   Makes about 1¹/₄ cups

3 ounces soft goat cheese
1 cup Basic Vinaigrette (opposite)

Place ingredients in a food processor. Purée until smooth. Stir before using.

Yogurt-Curry Dressing   Makes about 2¹/₃ cups

2 cups plain yogurt
2 tablespoons freshly squeezed
    orange juice
¹/₃ cup olive oil
1 tablespoon curry powder
Scant ¹/₂ teaspoon cayenne pepper
1 tablespoon honey
1 teaspoon finely grated orange
    zest, packed
Salt
Freshly ground black pepper

Whisk together until combined. Excellent on fruit salad.

ENTRÉES

Artichoke & Prosciutto Strata
148

Pesto, Mushroom
& Cheese Strata
149

Bun Bun Noodles
with Spicy Peanut Sauce
150

China Moon Shanghai Rice
151

Black Bean Chili
153

Tex-Mex Corn Bread Pudding
154

Curried Fried Rice
155

Mango Quesadillas
156

Alpbacher Gröstl
158

Turkey-Fried Hash
159

Scrapple
160

Tofu Scramble
161

Artichoke & Prosciutto Strata

Makes one 8-inch square pan

This voluptuous combination of flavorful ingredients comes my way from Beth Keegstra, an emergency room doctor and accomplished cook.

1/2 ounce dried porcini mushrooms

1/2 cup porcini soaking liquid

4 large eggs

3 cups half-and-half

1/2 teaspoon salt

1/4 teaspoon freshly ground pepper

About 8 cups (about 10 ounces by weight) cubed crusty bread (1 1/2 to 2 inches square)

1/2 cup fresh basil, cut into very thin strips (cut, then measured)

1/2 cup fresh dill, chopped

1 (6.5-ounce) jar marinated artichoke hearts, drained

3 ounces prosciutto, chopped into 1/2-inch-wide strips

1/2 cup grated Fontina Val d'Aosta cheese

4 ounces fresh goat cheese, crumbled

1/4 cup grated Parmigiano-Reggiano cheese

Soak the porcini in hot water to cover for about 30 minutes. Drain, reserving the liquid, and chop the mushrooms fine. Strain the liquid through a coffee filter or several layers of cheesecloth to remove any grit. Reserve 1/2 cup.

Beat together the eggs, half-and-half, porcini liquid, salt, and pepper until well blended. Adjust for seasoning. Place bread cubes in a large bowl and pour the egg mixture over it. Stir and let sit for 30 minutes, stirring occasionally.

Place half the bread cubes on the bottom of a lightly buttered 8-inch square pan. Layer over this all the basil and dill, all of the artichoke hearts, half the prosciutto, half the porcini, half the Fontina, and half the goat cheese. Cover with the other half of the bread cubes, and layer on the remaining ingredients in the same sequence. Sprinkle with the grated Parmigiano-Reggiano cheese and pour any remaining custard over the top.

Bake at 350°F for 1 hour, uncovered. If the top starts to brown too much, cover with foil. Let rest about 10 minutes before serving.

Pesto, Mushroom & Cheese Strata

Makes 6 to 8 servings

Strata means "layers" and the layers that follow create a rich and savory bread pudding. The point of the strata is that the whole should be more than the sum of its parts, which are often a little bit of this and that, and a lot of dry bread, eggs, and milk. Make this with any kind of leftover bread, crusts and all.

2 tablespoons unsalted butter

6 ounces (by weight) button
   mushrooms, sliced thinly

$1/2$ cup thinly sliced green onions

6 to 8 slices dry bread, with crust
   (about 10 ounces, enough to
   cover the bottom of an 8- by
   8-inch pan twice)

5 ounces grated sharp Cheddar
   or Gruyère cheese

5 large eggs

2 cups milk

2 tablespoons Pesto (page 141)

$1/4$ teaspoon Tabasco sauce

$3/4$ teaspoon salt

Freshly ground black pepper

In a small sauté pan, melt the butter, add mushrooms, and cook over medium-low heat for about 3 minutes, then add onions and continue cooking for 2 minutes more, until both are tender.

Place one layer of bread snugly in the bottom of an 8-inch square pan, sprinkle with the sautéed mushrooms and onions, then with the cheese.

Cube the remaining bread and evenly distribute in the pan.

Whisk together the remaining ingredients thoroughly and pour over the bread and cheese. Gently push the bread into the egg mixture. Cover pan tightly with plastic wrap and refrigerate at least 4 hours or overnight. Let stand at room temperature for 30 to 60 minutes before baking.

Preheat oven to 350°F. Remove plastic wrap and place the pan in the top third of the oven. Bake for 40 to 45 minutes, until the top is crunchy and brown. Let stand for 5 minutes before serving.

Bun Bun Noodles with Spicy Peanut Sauce

Makes 4 to 6 servings

This recipe was inspired by fond memories of one of the best Chinese noodle dishes I have ever tasted, those offered by my late friend Barbara Tropp at her China Moon Café. It combines five of my favorite ingredients in one dish: peanut butter, chile peppers, noodles, sesame oil, and soy sauce.

Customers really went wild for these noodles, often requesting the recipe and asking about the name. I must confess, the origin is a little embarrassing because I flippantly made up the name right before lunch one day.

10 ounces dry pasta—spaghetti or angel hair

1/4 cup smooth peanut butter (the most unadulterated brand available)

3 tablespoons sugar

1/4 cup low-salt soy sauce

1 teaspoon red pepper flakes

3 tablespoons toasted sesame oil

1 tablespoon minced garlic

3 tablespoons canola oil

Garnishes: julienned carrots and red peppers, green onions, toasted sesame seeds, roasted peanuts, fresh cilantro

In a large pot of boiling salted water, cook pasta until done, drain, and rinse with cold water until the noodles are cold. Let the noodles drain for about 10 minutes.

Whisk together the rest of the ingredients, except garnishes, until thoroughly blended. (If necessary, heat the mixture very *gently* and *briefly* to blend.) Toss the noodles with sauce.

Let stand at room temperature for at least 2 hours before serving. Refrigerate for longer storage, but no longer than 2 days. Toss the noodles before serving to distribute dressing.

To serve, place a mound of noodles on a plate and add your choice of any or all of the crunchy garnishes.

China Moon Shanghai Rice

Makes 3 to 4 servings

Barbara Tropp was chef/owner of the beloved China Moon Café in San Francisco, and the author of two extraordinary cookbooks on Chinese cuisine. (This recipe is adapted with permission from *China Moon Cookbook*). She considered this a "... wonderfully warm and soothing rice dish, very colorful and redolent of smoked bacon. A simple omelette or scrambled eggs would be the perfect accompaniment."

1 cup short-grain or medium-grain rice

3 tablespoons tiny cubes smoked bacon, fatty parts included (good-quality bacon, pancetta, or crumbled pork sausage can also be used)

1 1/2 teaspoons kosher salt (if sea or table is used, use only half as much)

1 tablespoon canola or peanut oil

1/3 cup finely sliced shallots

1 tablespoon Chinese rice wine or dry sherry

One or more of these garnishes: thinly cut green and white scallion rings, finely diced red bell peppers, or red Fresno chiles, finely julienned carrots, finely julienned snow peas, blanched hearts of baby Chinese cabbage

Wash rice repeatedly in several rinsings of cold water until the water runs clear. Drain well.

In a small skillet, add the bacon and 1/8 inch water, then bring to a simmer and cook until the cubes "seize up" and render some fat, about 2 minutes. Drain the juices into a cup measure and add enough hot water to equal 1 1/2 cups. Add the salt and stir to dissolve.

Heat a heavy 2–2 1/2-quart saucepan over moderate heat until hot. Glaze the bottom with oil, add the shallots and bacon, then stir gently until shallots are golden and very fragrant, adjusting the heat so they sizzle without scorching. Add the wine, stir about 10 seconds to burn off the alcohol, then add the rice and stir to mix.

Add the salted bacon water to the pan, stir well to combine, and bring to a simmer. Cover, reduce heat to the lowest possible setting (if using an electric stove, transfer the pot to a preheated low burner), and cook for 20 minutes without lifting the lid. Remove the pot from the stove and let it sit, undisturbed, for another 20 minutes.

Remove the lid, fluff the rice gently with a spatula to loosen it, then stir in the scallions and peppers or other garnishes, reserving some to sit prettily on top.

Black Bean Chili

Makes 8 generous servings

I simply couldn't omit this favorite, which also appears in my first book, *Cafe Beaujolais*. Next to waffles, it was our most popular dish. This version has fewer jalapeño chiles, but if you like a really spicy chili, by all means, add more.

When Julia Child came to visit, this is what she ordered. Naturally, the whole town knew she had come and everyone was curious about what she ordered. For months afterward, the sales of this dish were off the chart, and the kitchen turned out endless gallons of chili, barely keeping up with the demand.

I am indebted to Greens, the famous San Francisco vegetarian restaurant, for the original recipe.

4 cups dry black beans

2 tablespoons cumin seeds

2 tablespoons Beaujolais Blend Herbs* or dried oregano

2 cups finely chopped yellow onions

1 1/2 cups finely chopped green bell peppers

1 teaspoon minced garlic

1/2 cup olive oil

1 teaspoon cayenne pepper

1 1/2 tablespoons paprika

1 teaspoon salt

3 cups canned crushed whole tomatoes

1/3 cup finely chopped jalapeño chiles

1/2 pound Monterey Jack or Cheddar cheese, grated

Sour cream

1/2 cup finely chopped green onions

8 sprigs and/or 1/4 cup chopped cilantro

* Beaujolais Blend Herbs are available from Fuller's Fine Herbs (www.fullersfineherbs.com)

Sort through the beans; discard the funky ones and the small pebbles. (Our prep cook didn't like doing this either.) Rinse well. Place in a large pot and cover with water to several inches over the beans, cover, and bring to a boil.

Reduce the heat and cook for about 1 3/4 hours, or until tender. Water should always cover the beans, so add more if the beans start to peek through. When the beans are cooked, strain, reserving 1 cup of the cooking water. Add reserved cooking water back to the beans.

Toast the cumin seeds and Beaujolais Blend Herbs in a small pan at 325°F for about 10 minutes, until the fragrance is toasty.

Sauté the onions, green peppers, and garlic in the oil with the toasted cumin seeds and herbs, cayenne pepper, paprika, and salt for 10 minutes, or until the onions are soft. Add the tomatoes and chiles. Add this mixture to the beans and stir well.

To serve, place about 1/4 cup grated cheese in a warmed bowl, add a generous cup of beans, and dollop with a spoonful of sour cream. Sprinkle with 1 tablespoon green onions and cilantro.

Tex-Mex Corn Bread Pudding

Makes 4 to 6 servings

A corn bread surplus once haunted Cafe Beaujolais when leftover muffins accumulated in the freezer. After reaching critical mass (90% of the freezer was filled with muffins), my former husband and Beaujolais chef, Chris Kump, developed this recipe to cope with the problem.

The amount of croutons may seem excessive when first cut, but they reduce significantly when dried. Just see if you can resist nibbling! Try them as a garnish on Black Bean Chili (page 153) or on a salad.

To reheat, wrap in foil and place in a preheated 350°F oven for 15 minutes.

Half the Corn Bread recipe (page 40, using half for this recipe, and the rest for another dish)

1 1/2 cups (about 6 ounces) grated Monterey Jack or sharp Cheddar cheese

4 large eggs

2 egg yolks

1 teaspoon turmeric

3 cups warm milk

1/4 cup finely chopped fresh jalapeño peppers

1/2 cup chopped roasted or fresh red bell peppers

1/2 cup finely chopped green onions

1 1/2 teaspoons salt

2 teaspoons dried oregano (toasted at 300°F for 5 to 8 minutes)

1/4 teaspoon Tabasco sauce

Preheat oven to 300°F.

Cut corn bread into 3/4-inch cubes and spread in a single layer on a 10- by 15-inch pan. Bake for about 45 minutes until dry and lightly browned; stir occasionally.

Let cool. Place in a single layer in a lightly buttered 8-inch square pan. They will cover the entire bottom. Sprinkle with the cheese.

Turn the oven up to 375°F.

In a large bowl, mix together the eggs, yolks, and turmeric until well blended. Add the milk and remaining ingredients.

Pour the liquid evenly over the bread and cheese. Poke any escaping croutons below the surface so they soak up the custard.

Carefully place the pan into a 9- by 13-inch pan and pour boiling water into the larger pan, about halfway up the sides.

Bake for about 20 to 25 minutes, or until set in the center. When a knife inserted in the center comes out clean, the pudding is done. Let cool 5 minutes before serving.

Curried Fried Rice

Makes 2 servings

Rice, like cornmeal, is endlessly versatile and satisfying. To be honest, my idea of a wonderful meal is a huge serving of rice pudding, but rice in any form is something I enjoy. Garnish Daly, a former restaurateur via Cambridge, Massachusetts, and New York City, works these days as a grocer at Corners of the Mouth in Mendocino, volunteers at community fundraisers, and, in his spare time, does events with his old friends at the Hog Farm. He also taught my daughter how to professionally bag groceries when she was just six years old. But that's not all. He also makes a quick and easy curried fried rice dish, just the kind of food to make from leftovers in a few minutes.

2 large eggs

Canola oil

1 cup diced zucchini (1/4 inch) or your choice of red bell peppers, mushrooms, steamed green beans, and/or tofu

1 teaspoon minced garlic

2 to 3 teaspoons curry powder (make sure it's fresh and flavorful)

1/3 cup thinly sliced (cut on the diagonal) green onions

3 cups cooked cold rice (white, brown, or a mixture)

Salt

Toasted sesame oil

Coarsely chopped cilantro leaves

Beat eggs with 1 tablespoon water.

Heat an 8-inch nonstick pan, add 2 teaspoons oil, and when the oil is very hot, pour in the eggs. Stir quickly and cook until dry. Transfer to a bowl.

Heat a 10-inch nonstick pan, add 1 tablespoon oil, and when the oil is hot, add zucchini and turn heat down to medium. Season with a pinch or two of salt and sauté for 1 minute, stirring. Add garlic and curry powder, turn heat to low, and cook for another minute. Do not let it brown. Turn heat up and add green onions and rice. Stir to coat and heat through, and continue cooking for about 3 minutes. Mix in cooked egg and a few drops of sesame oil, heat, and then serve on warm plates. Garnish with cilantro leaves.

Mango Quesadillas

Makes 6 double-decker quesadillas

Even in a town as small as Mendocino (population 1,100), a long residence does not guarantee knowing everyone. It was inevitable, though, that Jude Lutge's path and mine would converge as we not only share a love for cooking, travel, and the written word, but we have also had restaurants. Jude, now a writer/editor/chef consultant/marketing director, was co-owner of the renowned Varsity Theatre Restaurant and Bar in Palo Alto, and founded Panache Catering in the Bay Area. This recipe comes from an earlier chapter in her multifaceted life.

12 medium-sized flour tortillas (about 6^1/$_2$-inch diameter)

1 pound firm pepper Jack cheese, coarsely grated

1 bunch cilantro, leaves only

1 large mango (or more, if you prefer), ripe but slightly firm, sliced about ^{1}/$_8$-inch thick (use a serrated knife)

Canola oil, about ^{1}/$_2$ to ^{3}/$_4$ tablespoon for each quesadilla

Place 6 tortillas on your work space. Divide the cheese equally among them, covering each tortilla to within 1/4 to 1/2 inch of the edge. Scatter with cilantro leaves and slices of mango. Cover each with another tortilla and press down lightly. These can be prepared to this point and set aside for up to 1 hour before last-minute cooking. Keep at room temperature on a cutting board or counter.

Heat a sauté pan large enough to hold one double-decker quesadilla. (If you have a crowd, keep several pans going.) Pour in the canola oil; it will barely coat the bottom of the pan. This small amount will get your tortillas deliciously crispy, but not oily. Make sure the pan is just hot enough. Ascertaining the exact amount of heat comes with experience and fiddling around. A proper adjustment keeps the pan hot enough to brown the tortillas toasty on each side without burning, allowing the cheese to melt, and the mango to get hot. At the right temperature, it takes only about 1 minute per side to cook. Before starting each tortilla, add a little oil as needed, and let it heat up for several seconds.

When tortilla is a deep rich brown on one side, flip over and cook until it browns on the other side. Remove to a cutting board. Let sit a minute before cutting in half, then cut each half into 3 triangles; alternatively, cut into quarters. Serve as soon as possible.

Alpbacher Gröstl

Makes 6 to 8 servings

Gröstl is an Austrian farmer's hash, a hearty mixture of potatoes and meat, flavored with caraway seed, and served with a fried egg or two. Any leftover meat makes a nice addition; so if you have chicken, bacon, or sausage, replace part of the beef or ham with it.

2 pounds boiled and chilled
  unpeeled potatoes

1 pound roast beef

1 pound smoked ham

4 tablespoons canola oil, or
  unsalted butter, or a mixture
  of the two

1 cup finely chopped onions

2 teaspoons caraway seeds

Salt

Freshly ground black pepper

1/4 cup minced parsley

Cut potatoes and meat into 3/4-inch cubes.

Over medium heat, fry the potatoes in a nonstick pan using 3 tablespoons of the oil or butter, until golden brown. This can take as long as 20 minutes.

In a separate pan, sauté the onion over medium heat in the remaining oil until golden brown, then add to the potatoes, along with the caraway seeds. Cook for another 2 to 3 minutes, and add the meat. Season with salt and pepper, sprinkle with parsley, and serve.

Turkey-Fried Hash

Thanksgiving is my favorite food holiday and stuffing is central to my happiness for this meal. I like to use the recipe from my *Cafe Beaujolais* cookbook and add luxurious ingredients, like Armagnac-soaked prunes and maple-glazed chestnuts. One year, after stuffing a large turkey and baking extra stuffing in a pan, I still had more than a gallon and a half left over. So much for my guess-timating ability. In an attempt to use up the leftovers, I dreamed up a hash and offered it the next day at the restaurant.

I had no idea how my customers would respond to this improvisation, but three hours later, not a speck remained! I give no quantities because everything here is flexible and depends on what you find in *your* refrigerator.

Small chunks of fresh pear
(about $1/2$ inch)

Unsalted butter

Cooked cubed potatoes

Leftover stuffing

Chopped roast turkey

Cooked crumbled spicy pork
sausage

Cranberry sauce

Minced parsley for garnish

Sauté pear in butter until soft; set aside.

Sauté potatoes until brown; set aside.

Mix together stuffing, turkey, sausage, pears, and a small amount of cranberry sauce. Add potatoes. Make patties about $1/2$- to $3/4$-inch thick and 3 inches in diameter, and fry in butter using a nonstick pan.

Cook over medium-high heat, until browned on both sides, and garnish with parsley. Serve with fried eggs.

Scrapple

Makes one 8-inch loaf pan

Scrapple is a Pennsylvania Dutch dish made originally from cornmeal mush (or sometimes oats and barley) and, well, what is often called "unmentionable pork parts." If you want to read some really funny descriptions and reactions to this dish, visit a few sites on the Internet. Put the word "scrapple" into your favorite search engine and get ready to laugh.

10 ounces ground pork or sage sausage

3/4 teaspoon salt

3/4 teaspoon freshly ground pepper

1/2 teaspoon dried sage (omit if using sage sausage)

1/8 teaspoon cayenne

1/8 teaspoon dried savory

4 cups water

1 teaspoon salt

1 teaspoon Beaujolais Blend Herbs* or dried oregano

1 1/4 cups polenta

Cornmeal for dredging

Canola oil and/or unsalted butter

* Beaujolais Blend Herbs are available from Fuller's Fine Herbs (www.fullersfineherbs.com)

Crumble the sausage and cook in a pan over medium heat, stirring until no pinkness is left. Add the salt, pepper, sage, cayenne, and savory. Set aside; do not drain fat.

Bring the water to a boil in a 2-quart pot; add salt and herbs. Slowly sprinkle in polenta, stirring constantly. Once the polenta begins to spit at you, reduce the heat and stir for another 10 minutes. Stir in the sausage, fat included, and mix until well distributed.

Pour into an 8- by 4-inch loaf pan and smooth top immediately. Place plastic wrap directly on the surface and refrigerate until chilled thoroughly, several hours or overnight. Run a knife around the outside of the scrapple and turn the loaf out onto a board.

Pour 1 cup of cornmeal into a pan.

Slice loaf into 12 to 16 pieces, dredge both sides of each slice in cornmeal.

Heat a 10-inch nonstick pan and add 2 teaspoons oil/butter. Once hot, carefully place the slices of scrapple in the pan. After 15 seconds, turn the heat down to medium-high and cook until browned and crispy. Flip, and cook on other side.

Serve on warm plates with maple syrup. Repeat with remaining slices or refrigerate until needed. Will keep up to 4 days.

Sage Sausage

3/4 teaspoon salt

3/4 teaspoon black pepper

1/2 teaspoon dried sage

Pinch of cayenne

Pinch of savory

10 ounces unseasoned ground sausage

Mix together all seasonings, then combine with sausage.

Tofu Scramble

Makes 4 servings

This breakfast creation was wildly popular at Cafe Beaujolais. It's a good alternative to eggs, with the addition of other healthy ingredients. Customize the dish according to vegetable availability.

Tofu Mix

2 cups crumbled firm tofu

2 tablespoons salsa, plus about
    1/2 cup for garnish

1 tablespoon toasted ground
    cumin seed

3/4 teaspoon salt

1/4 to 1/2 teaspoon cayenne pepper

Vegetable Mix

2 tablespoons olive or canola oil

3 cups boiled and chilled unpeeled
    potatoes, cubed (1/2 inch)

3 cups vegetables (total):
    blanched carrots, broccoli,
    thinly sliced green onions, corn
    kernels, roasted red peppers,
    cubed (1/4 inch) zucchini/bell
    peppers, thinly sliced celery

2 teaspoons minced garlic or
    8 cloves roasted garlic
    (page 102)

Salt

Freshly ground pepper

About 1 cup hot Black Bean Chili
    (page 153)

1/3 cup coarsely chopped fresh
    cilantro

Warmed tortillas

Combine ingredients for tofu mix. Set aside.

Heat a 10-inch nonstick pan, add 2 tablespoons olive or canola oil, then add the potatoes. Cook over medium-high heat until browned, about 10 minutes, add the bell pepper and minced garlic (roasted garlic is added later in recipe). Cook, stirring to prevent garlic from burning, until pepper is tender, about 5 minutes. Add celery and cook for 1 minute, then add remaining vegetables, the roasted garlic, and heat through. Add tofu mix and stir to combine. Heat through and adjust for seasoning.

To serve, divide vegetable mixture among 4 warm plates. Add a dollop of Black Bean Chili and sprinkle with cilantro. Pass additional salsa and serve with tortillas.

DESSERTS

Easy Homemade Yogurt: Plain,
Chocolate & Caramel
164

Black & White Soufflé
165

Berry-filled Custard Crêpes
166

Warm Berries & Peaches
with Shortcake Biscuits
& Whipped Cream
168

Baked Blintzes   170

Apple Butter Bread Pudding
171

Cream Cheese & Jam
Bread Pudding
172

Cherry Clafouti   173

Strawberry-Rhubarb Pie   174

Chris's Butterscotch-Walnut Pie
175

Pie Crust   176

Brown Sugar Thins   177

Calas   178

Ginger Shortbread   179

Apricot-Pecan Caramel
Shortbread   180

Almond-filled Butter Cake
181

Mutti's Marble Cake   183

Anne Fox's Fabulous
Pumpkin Pie
184

Mom's Almost-Unbearably-
Delicious Chocolate Fudge
185

Chocolate Sin   186

Crema Catalana   187

Clay's Almond Cake   188

Ginger-Apple Crumb Torte   189

Easy Homemade Yogurt: Plain, Chocolate & Caramel

Makes as much as you wish

No need for a fancy yogurt machine (although it helps to maintain the constant temperature required). My mom makes this all the time and it always turns out right. What I find so fascinating is that you need such an incredibly tiny amount of yogurt starter to create a new batch.

As much milk as you want, whole, low-fat, or nonfat

A little plain yogurt as starter

For chocolate yogurt: 1 generous tablespoon Mom's Cocoa Syrup (page 193), or 1 ounce semisweet chocolate, for every 2 cups milk used

For caramel yogurt: 6 caramels for every 2 cups milk used

Scald the milk to a temperature of 185°F. Cool to 115°F and strain into clean jars. For each cup of milk, add 1/4 teaspoon yogurt and stir well. Place lids on the jars and set into a water bath at about 115°F. Cover the water bath container to hold in the heat as much as possible. You can drape a towel or place a lid over it.

Set the entire water bath in the oven (or any other place in which you can maintain a temperature of between 110°F and 115°F). If you have an electric oven, turn it on for between 30 and 60 seconds, then turn it off. In a gas oven, the pilot light may be enough. The trick is to try to keep the temperature constant within this range for between 3 1/2 and 5 hours. After 5 hours, the yogurt begins to "go tart."

Don't disturb the yogurt while it is setting. When it is done, it will have the texture of soft custard. It becomes firmer after refrigeration. The watery whey that floats to the top can be stirred back in.

For chocolate yogurt: Stir in Mom's Cocoa Syrup or 1 ounce melted semisweet chocolate after scalding the milk, or use ready-made chocolate milk, which has to be intensely chocolate flavored or the finished product will taste wimpy. Proceed with the recipe.

For caramel yogurt: Stir in the caramels after scalding the milk. Proceed with the recipe.

Black & White Soufflé

Makes enough for 4 to 5 servings

For dessert, nothing is more impressive than a towering puff of chocolate cloud brought to the table amid "oohs" and "aahs." Served with whipped cream or a custard sauce, it's truly a taste of heaven. Use the very best chocolate available. For the white, which is not actually chocolate at all, the only kind I use is Callebaut from Belgium.

Unsalted butter, softened, for buttering the mold

White sugar for the mold

5 ounces semisweet chocolate, finely chopped, and melted

3 ounces white chocolate, finely chopped, and melted

1/4 cup milk

1/2 cup white sugar, divided into 1/3 cup and remainder

6 egg yolks, at room temperature

Pinch of salt

6 egg whites, at room temperature

1/2 teaspoon lemon juice

Whipped Cream Topping

3/4 cup heavy whipping cream

1 tablespoon powdered sugar

1/2 teaspoon vanilla extract

Preheat the oven to 350°F.

Prepare a 7-inch soufflé mold by buttering generously with softened butter and sprinkling with sugar. Tear off a strip of foil (28 inches), fold in half lengthwise, butter and sugar it, and wrap it around the mold so that it extends beyond the top of the mold by 4 inches. Secure with a paper clip, and tie tightly with string.

Whisk together the milk, 1/3 cup of the sugar, and egg yolks until well blended. Divide this mixture, pouring a third into a medium-sized bowl and two-thirds into another.

With an electric mixer, beat the egg whites with the salt until very foamy, then add the lemon juice. When the peaks are almost stiff, add the remaining sugar and beat about another 15 seconds until the peaks stand up when the beaters are removed from the whites.

Moving quickly, blend the white chocolate into the one-third egg mixture and the dark chocolate into the two-thirds egg mixture. An electric beater is necessary to blend the white chocolate thoroughly.

Using two different rubber spatulas, fold about one-third of the whites into the white mixture, and two-thirds of the whites into the dark mixture. Pour three-quarters of the dark chocolate mixture into the mold, then all of the white, then the remaining dark directly over the white.

Place in the oven and bake, undisturbed, for about 45 to 50 minutes. The soufflé will have risen; the top will be crusty but still jiggly.

Remove from the oven and bring directly to the table. Remove the foil collar and serve, passing whipped cream or custard sauce. The soufflé should still be soft, even somewhat saucelike, in the center.

For the Whipped Cream Topping: Whip the cream, sugar, and vanilla together only until soft peaks form. Do not overwhip.

Berry-filled Custard Crêpes

Makes 6 servings of 2 crêpes each

A package of crêpes should always be found in your freezer. During berry season, a warm crêpe wrapped around the berries of your choice and sprinkled with a little vanilla sugar, finished with a dot of crème fraîche or yogurt—a salute to simplicity and perfection. The first few crêpes usually look less than perfect, offering an opportunity to fine-tune the thickness of the batter (thin, as needed, with a few drops of water) and the heat. Once you get a rhythm going, you won't want to stop. It's really fun! Crêpes, well wrapped in plastic wrap, then placed in a sealed plastic bag, will keep a month or so in the freezer.

Batter   Makes about 12 crêpes

3 large eggs

1 cup, minus 2 tablespoons milk

1 teaspoon white sugar

$^1/_2$ cup water

$^1/_4$ teaspoon salt

3 tablespoons canola oil

1 cup white flour

Melted unsalted butter or canola oil for greasing the pan

In a blender, mix all the ingredients, except the butter, for 30 seconds. Strain through a sieve into a container. Stir, cover, and refrigerate for at least 2 hours before using.

When you're ready to make the crêpes, stir the batter. Heat an 8-inch nonstick pan over medium heat until a drop of water "skates" across the surface. Using a pastry brush, lightly grease the pan with the melted butter or oil and pour in about 3 tablespoons of batter, tilting the pan in all directions so the batter is evenly distributed. If there is too much, pour the excess back into the container. Crêpes should be very thin, about $^1/_{16}$-inch thick.

Cook until the edge of the crêpe is lightly browned, about 45 seconds. Loosen with a heat-proof spatula, and use your fingers to grab the edge and flip it over. Cook for about 20 seconds more and slide out of the pan onto a waiting plate. Repeat, stacking the crêpes. Let cool thoroughly.

To store, separate the crêpes into whatever number works best for your needs, cover tightly in plastic wrap, and refrigerate for up to 3 days. To keep longer, freeze. Allow frozen crêpes to defrost in the refrigerator.

Filling

4 ounces (by weight) natural
   cream cheese

2 tablespoons heavy whipping
   cream

2 egg yolks

2 teaspoons white sugar

2 cups berries

About 1 tablespoon melted
   unsalted butter

$1/2$ cup berry jam

$1/2$ cup light red wine

Preheat the oven to 325°F.

Beat the cream cheese until smooth, and then add the cream, egg yolks, and sugar. *Carefully* fold in the berries with a rubber spatula; try to keep intact.

Ladle a generous $1/4$ cup of this mixture down the center of each crêpe and fold the sides of the crêpe over the middle. Place the crêpes, seam side down, into 4 individual lightly buttered ovenproof serving dishes. If some of the mixture spills out, push it back in with a spoon.

Bring the jam and wine to a boil, turn down heat to medium, and cook for about 2 minutes. Cool slightly and pour over crêpes.

Bake for 10 to 15 minutes until heated through, garnish with an edible flower or sprig of mint, and serve.

Too Much of a Good Thing Is . . . Wonderful

When I was growing up, my mom would sometimes make Hungarian crêpes, *palacsinta*, fill them with apricot or prune jam, and dust them with powdered sugar. The magnificent cuisine of the Austro-Hungarian empire, which I had heard tales about from my dad whose parents were from Hungary, became very real when I lived in Austria. Besides the poppy seed pastries, nothing excited me more than the crêpes, which often enveloped elaborate ice cream concoctions. Various flavors of exceptional ice cream, fruit sauces and syrups, and, of course, whipped cream, arranged with flair on lovely plates, made such desserts unforgettable.

Warm Berries & Peaches with Shortcake Biscuits & Whipped Cream

Makes 6 generous servings

This is a hedonist's reverie, a dessert that pays homage to ripe fruits of the season paired with a rich pastry, a little alcohol, and some whipped cream. A moment of silence, please.

Use the freshest fruit you can find, and the most delicious *eau-de-vie* (unsweetened fruit brandy) obtainable. My favorite is Aqua Perfecta made by St. George Spirits (www.stgeorgespirits.com). How intense is it? Well, brandy made from 30 pounds of fruit is concentrated into 1 bottle. Although it won't satisfy any nutritional requirements, it is a restorative, chilled and savored slowly. Have a glass while the biscuits are baking.

Make the biscuits right before you use them. They are absolutely fabulous when absolutely fresh.

Fruit Mixture

2 cups blueberries

2 tablespoons white sugar

1 tablespoon lemon juice

$1/2$ teaspoon cornstarch

Pinch of salt

2 small or 1 large peach, peeled, and cut into eighths

3 cups raspberries

2 tablespoons raspberry eau-de-vie

Shortcake Biscuits

2 cups flour

6 tablespoons of sugar

1 tablespoon baking powder

$3/4$ teaspoon salt

$1/4$ cup unsalted butter, cut into 1-teaspoon-sized pieces, and frozen

2 cups and 2 tablespoons heavy whipping cream, divided

1 egg yolk

1 teaspoon vanilla extract, divided

To prepare the fruit: Combine the blueberries, 2 tablespoons sugar, lemon juice, cornstarch, and salt in a non-aluminum saucepan. (Aluminum reacts with the acid in the fruit and creates a peculiar taste.)

Bring to a boil and reduce the heat, simmering until the mixture thickens and a sauce forms, about 10 minutes. Stir occasionally to prevent sticking. Add the peaches and cook for 1 minute, then remove from heat, and gently fold in the raspberries and eau-de-vie. Set aside.

To make the biscuits: Preheat oven to 375°F. In a food processor, place the flour, 2 tablespoons sugar, baking powder, and salt. Blend briefly. Add the butter and pulse until the butter is the size of peas.

Pour mixture into a bowl, add 1 cup of the cream, and combine with a fork until moistened. Immediately turn out onto a lightly floured board and knead about 10 times. Small lumps of butter should be visible.

Roll out to a $3/4$-inch thickness. Keep dough in a square shape. Cut into 6 pieces and place on an ungreased cookie sheet.

Mix the egg yolk with 2 tablespoons of cream and $1/2$ teaspoon vanilla, and brush on the tops of the biscuits. Sprinkle with 2 tablespoons sugar.

Bake for 15 to 20 minutes or until golden brown.

To the remaining 1 cup whipping cream, add the remaining 2 tablespoons sugar and $1/2$ teaspoon vanilla extract. Beat only till soft peaks form. Refrigerate.

To assemble: When cool, split the biscuits and place the bottom half of each into a bowl. Add one-sixth of the berry mixture, and garnish with a dollop of whipped cream. Place the tops on, slightly off-center, and serve immediately.

Take Two Schnaps and Call Me in the Morning

When I lived in Austria, I was delighted to discover how much a part of the culture *schnaps* (brandy distilled from fermented fruits) is, since I have a real taste for it. Some farming families still have the right, conferred by the eighteenth-century monarch Empress Maria Theresa, to produce a limited amount of schnaps on-site. Schnaps are not only made from the more familiar stone fruits, but also from Alpine herbs, berries, pears, and even a kind of turnip. Some are an acquired taste. The use of schnaps as a *digestif almost* brings it into the health-food category, especially considering that some kinds are specifically used for medicinal purposes. That's why locals use the expression "Es ist Medizin."

Baked Blintzes

Makes 4 servings of 2 blintzes each

I love to serve and eat fried blintzes, but they require a gentle touch and are a pain in the neck to make when you are under pressure, as I often was in the restaurant. It occurred to me that baking them might be a simpler approach. While not as decadent as the fried version, they are awfully good and better for you, since the butter is kept to a minimum.

Individual baking dishes are necessary as hot blintzes are unwieldy to serve.

14 ounces ricotta cheese

1/2 pound natural cream cheese

1 egg yolk

Finely grated zest of 1 lemon

Pinch of freshly ground nutmeg

Pinch of cinnamon

1/2 teaspoon vanilla extract

2 1/2 tablespoons white sugar

8 Crêpes (page 166)

About 2 tablespoons melted unsalted butter

Sour cream for garnish

Fruit: Caramelized Applesauce (page 10), fresh berries, jam

Preheat the oven to 350°F.

Blend together the ricotta, cream cheese, egg yolk, lemon zest, nutmeg, cinnamon, vanilla, and sugar. Place the 8 crêpes on a work space and divide the filling among them, about 1/3 cup each, placing the filling in a strip across the middle.

Roll up and place, seam side down, into 4 individual lightly buttered baking dishes. Brush tops lightly with melted butter and bake for about 15 minutes, until heated through. Garnish and serve.

Apple Butter Bread Pudding

Makes 6 to 8 servings

The irreverent Neil O'Brien, who worked at the Cafe for two years, absolutely loved this dessert but apparently felt he wasn't getting enough at meals. He noticed that most of the staff preferred it warm, while his preference was for cold. Gradually, *somehow* it wound up being served cold as a matter of course. Until his ploy was discovered, he got all he wanted. Have I mentioned how much like a family we were?

5 ounces stale bread/pastries (we used an assortment of odds and ends, cut into 3/4-inch to 1-inch cubes, crusts left on)

3/4 cup apple butter (if you only have applesauce, mix 1 1/2 cups with 1 tablespoon sugar and 1 teaspoon cinnamon, pour into a 9- by 13-inch pan, and bake at 350°F for 1 hour, stirring frequently, until it thickens and reduces to 3/4 cup)

4 large eggs

Pinch of salt

2 1/2 cups milk

1/2 cup brown sugar

1 teaspoon vanilla extract

1/2 teaspoon cinnamon

1/4 teaspoon freshly grated nutmeg

Preheat the oven to 350°F.

Place the bread in the bottom of an 8- by 8-inch pan and distribute blobs of apple butter over the surface.

Beat together the remaining ingredients.

Pour the custard over the bread, dunking the bread to ensure it is soaked. Set the pan into a larger, 9- by 13-inch, pan and fill the outer pan with hot water, halfway up the sides. Do this near the stove to avoid sloshing and burning yourself.

Bake for 50 to 55 minutes. Test for doneness with a knife inserted into the center. When it comes out clean, remove the pudding from the oven and let cool.

Cream Cheese & Jam Bread Pudding

Makes 8 servings

In my first book, *Cafe Beaujolais,* I included a recipe for a cream cheese and jam omelette. More than a few people told me they thought it was weird. All I can say is that one person's weird is another person's wonderful. So if this bread pudding sounds good to you, please make it, and use the best jam you can find.

3 slices dry, white bread

4 ounces (by weight) natural
  cream cheese

1/3 cup seedless raspberry jam

2 1/2 cups whole milk

1 teaspoon vanilla extract

5 large eggs, beaten

1/2 cup white sugar

1/4 teaspoon freshly grated nutmeg

1/4 teaspoon salt

Preheat the oven to 325°F.

Spread the cream cheese, then the jam, over the bread slices. Cut into 1-inch squares. This is a sloppy procedure. Place the squares, cream-cheese-and-jam side down, into an 8-inch square pan. Whisk together the remaining ingredients and pour over the bread. Push the bread into the custard mixture to soak.

Place the pan into a larger, 9- by 13-inch, pan and fill the outer pan with hot water, halfway up the sides.

Bake for about 50 to 55 minutes. Test for doneness with a knife inserted into the center. When it comes out clean, remove the pudding from the oven, and let cool on a rack for 1 hour.

Cherry Clafouti

Makes 4 to 5 servings

I think of clafouti as a very French version of a refined cobbler. Although I've never been a fan of cobbler (usually too bready and heavy), I love clafouti. Our kitchen staff used to call this "cherry clawfoot." Properly pronounced, it comes out "claw-foo-*tee*." It is especially good with cherries, but also lends itself to other pitted fruits, as well as to apples and pears. However, bananas or canned fruit cocktail are forbidden. Canned Fruit Cocktail Clafouti would definitely set already tenuous Franco-American relations back *another* forty years.

3 large eggs

1/2 cup white sugar

1 teaspoon vanilla

1 1/2 cups half-and-half

Pinch of salt

2/3 cup white flour (measured, then sifted)

1 1/3 cups pitted cherries

3 tablespoons melted unsalted butter

Powdered sugar

Preheat the oven to 400°F (375°F, if you are using a glass baking dish).

In a medium-sized bowl, beat the eggs and sugar with a whisk until the mixture whitens, about 1 minute. Add the vanilla, half-and-half, salt, and flour and whisk until smooth. If lumps form, pour through a strainer and stir to blend.

Combine half of the batter with cherries in a separate bowl and stir gently to combine.

Pour the cherry mixture into a buttered 8-inch pie plate or 8-inch square pan. Bake for 15 minutes. Meanwhile, whisk the butter into the remaining batter. The butter will congeal, but don't worry. Pour over the partially baked clafouti and return to the oven for another 10 to 15 minutes, until golden brown.

Remove from oven and let cool for 10 minutes. Sprinkle with powdered sugar and serve.

Strawberry-Rhubarb Pie

Makes 8 servings

Strawberries and rhubarb are a classic combination, and the crumble topping adds a nice flavor-and-texture complement. Chris Kump introduced this recipe to Cafe Beaujolais, and it became a menu mainstay for several months each year.

Be sure to place the pie on the lowest rack of the oven, at least for the first half of the baking time, to prevent the topping and crust edge from burning. Use foil for protection, as needed.

1³/4 cups strawberries, quartered

1/4 to 1/3 cup white sugar, depending on the sweetness of the berries

1³/4 cups Rhubarb Glop (page 14)

3 large eggs, beaten

1 prebaked Pie Crust (page 176)

1¹/2 to 2 cups Crumble Topping (below)

Preheat the oven to 350°F.

Toss the strawberries with the sugar.

Add the Glop to the eggs and mix well. Stir in the strawberries. Pour into the pie shell. Sprinkle generously with Crumble Topping so that no filling is visible.

Bake for 1¹/4 hours, starting on the lower rack, until the center is set and the topping is golden brown.

Crumble Topping

1/2 cup dry bread crumbs

1/2 cup coarsely chopped hazelnuts, or walnuts, or a combination of the two

1/4 cup unsweetened shredded coconut

1/3 cup brown sugar

1/3 cup white flour

1/3 cup butter, in 1/2-inch cubes

Mix together all ingredients, except for the butter. Blend in the butter by hand, or with an electric mixer, until the mixture holds its shape when you grab a handful.

Chris's Butterscotch-Walnut Pie

Makes 1 pie that serves 9 to 10

Granted, I am a pushover for desserts with caramel. You may ask, "Is this morning food?" Don't ask. It's just too good to omit. Besides, some of the gooey breakfast treats, such as bear claws and sticky buns, come from the same family tree as this pie.

Break down the steps of this recipe so you can make it as you have time. The sauce and the crust can be made ahead, then you can throw everything together at the last minute.

2 cups Butterscotch Sauce (below)
1/2 cup heavy whipping cream
3 large eggs, lightly beaten
1/2 teaspoon vanilla extract
1 cup walnut pieces, toasted
1 tablespoon white flour
1 prebaked Pie Crust (page 176)

Preheat the oven to 350°F.

Combine the sauce, cream, eggs, and vanilla.

Toss the walnuts with the flour and sprinkle over the bottom of the pie shell. Pour the filling over the walnuts, which will rise to the top.

Bake for 40 to 50 minutes, until set in the center. Allow to cool on a rack.

Butterscotch Sauce

1/2 cup unsalted butter, melted
1 cup dark brown sugar
2/3 cup light corn syrup
1/3 cup heavy whipping cream

Boil the butter, sugar, and corn syrup together over medium-low heat for 8 to 10 minutes, stirring occasionally. Watch the pot carefully. It will want to boil over but you let it know who's boss by reducing the heat as needed. Allow to cool for 15 minutes, then stir in the cream.

The sauce will keep quite a while in the refrigerator. If it should crystallize (like honey), scoop it into a saucepan and boil gently for 2 minutes.

Pie Crust

Makes one 9-inch crust

All too often, pies with great potential end up being submerged under (and over) a soggy crust. After testing countless recipes, we discovered Richard Sax's marvelous book, *Old Fashioned Desserts* (Irena Chalmers Cookbooks, Inc., 1983), a must for anyone who is serious about baking delicious desserts. The method of forming the shell may sound a bit complicated, but you will surely get the hang of it after one or two tries.

1 cup, plus 2 tablespoons white flour

1/4 teaspoon salt

1 teaspoon white sugar

5 tablespoons unsalted butter, cut into small pieces, and frozen

1 1/2 tablespoons shortening, frozen

1 tablespoon ice water

Place the flour, salt, and sugar into a food processor and combine. Add the butter and shortening and pulse until they are cut into the flour, about 3 seconds. Add the ice water and process for another 2 or 3 seconds, the less the better, since pie dough becomes tough when handled excessively.

Turn out the dough onto a lightly floured board and press into a flat disk, about 4 inches in diameter and 1 inch thick. Wrap in plastic wrap and refrigerate for several hours, or freeze for use later.

Remove the dough from the refrigerator and place it on a lightly floured board. Use a rolling pin to flatten the dough, hitting down and toward the center of the circle. Move the dough in quarter turns during this step. When the dough is 1/2 inch thick, roll it out and continue to turn in order to ensure an even surface. Add as little extra flour as possible. Use a brush to dust flour onto the surface, if needed.

When the dough is 1/8 inch thick, lift, and place into a pie pan. Crimp the edges, trimming any excess dough. Prick with a fork, then freeze for at least 30 minutes.

When ready to bake, preheat the oven to 425°F. Place a large piece of foil over the surface of the dough, then place beans or rice on the foil to weigh down the dough. Keep the foil from touching the crimped edges. Bake for 10 minutes on the top shelf of the oven until the top border is set and looks more like crust than dough. Carefully remove the weight, then the foil, and lower the heat to 375°F. Return the pie shell to the bottom rack in the oven and bake for 15 minutes, or until the entire crust is a light golden brown. If the edges start to brown too much, cover with foil. Remove from the oven when done and let cool briefly on a rack.

Brown Sugar Thins

Makes about 8 dozen cookies

I try to have this dough on hand in the freezer at all times, ready to whip out, and bake to order. It's fun and easy to make with kids.

1 1/2 cups unsalted butter, softened

1 1/2 cups firmly packed light or dark brown sugar

2 large eggs

2 1/2 cups white flour

1/2 teaspoon salt

1 teaspoon vanilla extract

Preheat oven to 350°F.

Cream together the butter and sugar until fluffy. Add the eggs and beat to combine. Mix in the flour, salt, and vanilla. Chill for at least 1 hour.

Drop 12 scant teaspoons onto an ungreased cookie sheet and bake for about 8 minutes, until the edges are brown.

Cool for 30 seconds before removing from pan. Using a metal spatula, lift each cookie off the pan carefully and place on a cooling rack. Let cool thoroughly, then transfer to an airtight container, and/or your mouth.

Read This Quietly

Although it is a cliché that one does not disturb or distress a soufflé while it is cooking, it is a cliché that's actually true. This is *not* the time to practice your folk dancing or knife juggling in the kitchen. In fact, when my mom used to make soufflés, she grew nearly hysterical if anyone closed a door in the house. Okay, they may not be *that* delicate, but why take the chance? A fallen soufflé will still taste good, but it is rather dense and, well, unsoufflélike.

Calas

Makes 25

Peter Kump, my former father-in-law, once told me that calas used to be sold on street corners in New Orleans, where deep-fried foods are famous. Experiments to lighten the recipe created something I really like. Be sure to use a candy thermometer to determine, and monitor, the correct oil temperature.

6 cups water

1 teaspoon salt

1 cup uncooked long-grain white rice

1/3 cup cornstarch

1/3 cup cake flour

2 teaspoons baking powder

1/4 teaspoon salt

1/2 teaspoon cinnamon

Pinch of freshly grated nutmeg

1/3 cup white sugar

1/3 cup beaten eggs

Canola oil for frying

Extra cinnamon for sprinkling

Extra sugar for sprinkling

Bring water to a boil. Add salt and the rice. Boil, uncovered, over medium-high heat for about 15 minutes, or until very tender. Drain, rinse with cold water, and drain again. Set aside.

Sift together the cornstarch, cake flour, baking powder, salt, cinnamon, and nutmeg. Set aside.

In a separate bowl, whisk together the sugar and eggs until pale yellow, about 1 minute, and stir in the rice to coat well. Gradually whisk in the flour mixture.

In a deep, heavy pot, heat about 2 inches of oil to 375°F. Use a candy thermometer to determine the temperature. Do not let the oil overheat! Use a spoon to scoop a heaping tablespoon of the batter and *carefully* slide it into the hot oil. Take care not to drop it in or the hot oil will splatter. Fry for about 25 seconds, or until golden brown all over, turning as necessary. Drain on paper towels, sprinkle with cinnamon and sugar, and serve immediately.

Ginger Shortbread

Makes 12 pieces

Shortbread seems to be a cookie that everyone likes. Buttery and flavorful, what's *not* to like? Here's a variation that incorporates another delicious flavor, the spiciness of ginger. Traditional shortbread is a pale yellow, but I prefer it delicately browned on the edges. This is another dough you can freeze and then bake when needed.

2 ounces (by weight) candied ginger

$2/3$ cup unsalted butter, softened

$1/2$ cup powdered sugar (sifted, then measured)

$2/3$ cup white flour (sifted, then measured)

$3/4$ cup cornstarch (sifted, then measured)

Pinch of salt

Preheat oven to 325°F.

In a food processor, place the ginger and butter and process until the ingredients are well blended, about 30 seconds to 1 minute, depending on the firmness of the ginger.

Transfer to a medium-sized bowl and add remaining ingredients with a wooden spoon or electric mixer until thoroughly combined.

Pat the dough evenly into an 8-inch round pan, using a rubber spatula to scrape the dough off your hands. It should be soft and messy.

Using a fork held vertically, divide the circle into 12 wedge-shaped sections. Then use the fork tines to press a pattern of lines around the outside of the circle, about half an inch long.

Bake for 30 to 35 minutes, shifting the pan if necessary to prevent uneven baking.

When done, remove from the oven. Use a fork to re-score the lines as they will have partially fused during baking. Cool on a rack. If you can hide them quickly enough, these cookies keep well in an airtight container.

Apricot-Pecan Caramel Shortbread

Makes 20 rich pieces

Sometimes you want to eat something with no redeeming social or nutritional value. In this book (with no shortage of such recipes), this is the absolute "something." Another recipe from the caramel-encrusted kitchen of Barbara Holzrichter, sugar sorceress.

1²/3 cups Caramel Sauce
  (page 56)

1 cup chopped moist dried
  apricots (not the leathery kind)

1 cup chopped, lightly toasted
  pecans

²/3 cup unsalted butter, softened

¹/4 cup white sugar

1³/4 cups white flour

Pinch of salt

Preheat the oven to 350°F.

In the top of a double boiler, or over very low heat, warm the caramel sauce and when melted, stir in the apricots and pecans. Set aside.

In a bowl, beat the butter with the sugar until light. Then mix in the flour and salt to combine. Press the dough evenly into an 8-inch-square pan. Bake for 20 minutes, then remove from the oven and pour the caramel mixture over the top. Return to the oven and bake for another 12 to 15 minutes. Remove, let cool on a rack for 5 minutes, then run a knife around the outside of the "cookie" to prevent the caramel from gluing itself to the side of the pan, making removal impossible. When cooler, cut into a great many pieces.

Almond-filled Butter Cake

Makes 1 cake that serves 12 to 16

This authentic Dutch recipe is from Jocelyn Kamstra Sugrue, whose role as kitchen manager was, for many years, crucial to the restaurant's smooth operation. She also is a magnificent cook.

Don't expect a light and fluffy cake from this recipe. It is anything but. Rather, the texture is dense and the cake rich, best served in thin slices with a cup of full-bodied coffee. Store unrefrigerated for up to a week, although the odds are slim any will still be left by then.

Butter Cake Crust

$2^2/3$ cups white flour

$1^1/3$ cups white sugar

$1^1/3$ cups cold unsalted butter

$1/2$ teaspoon salt

1 large egg

Almond Filling

1 cup finely chopped almonds

$1/2$ cup white sugar

$2^1/2$ teaspoons finely grated
 lemon zest

1 large egg, slightly beaten

12 whole almonds for garnish

Preheat the oven to 325°F.

Grease a 9-inch or 10-inch springform pan. Combine all the crust ingredients in a mixing bowl. Using an electric mixer or food processor, blend until dough forms. Chill for 10 minutes. Divide the dough in half. Spread one half on the bottom of the prepared pan. Refrigerate the other half.

In a small bowl, combine all the filling ingredients, except for the whole almonds. Spread the filling over the dough in the pan to within $1/2$ inch of the edge. Between two pieces of waxed paper, press or roll the remaining dough into a 9-inch or 10-inch circle. Remove the top layer of waxed paper and turn the dough over the filling. Remove the remaining waxed paper and press the dough into place. Garnish with 12 almonds in a pleasing pattern.

Place in the oven with a cookie sheet on the lower rack to catch any spillage. Bake in the center of the oven for 60 to 70 minutes, until evenly browned. Be careful not to underbake. Remove from oven and cool on a metal rack for 15 minutes, then remove sides from pan and cool completely. Keep tightly covered, but do not refrigerate.

Mutti's Marble Cake

Makes 1 cake that serves 10 to 12

For years, I had kept a scrap of paper in my recipe file. On it were the ingredients for a cake written in a faded European script, with no instructions. This "recipe," from Elsa Kent, was given to me by her daughter, Laura Katz, who said, "You're the great cook— *you* figure it out."

Daunted by this challenge and overwhelmed at a certain point by recipe-testing for an earlier version of this book, I gave the crumpled piece of paper to pastry wizard Chris Kump, and a few hours later he emerged with a delicious, elegant, and refined marble cake. I have since tweaked it a bit more and discovered that the flavor is enhanced by letting the cooled cake sit, well wrapped in plastic wrap for a few hours or overnight, before serving.

1/4 cup unsweetened cocoa (I use Scharffen Berger)

3 tablespoons milk

1 2/3 cups white sugar, divided

1 cup unsalted butter, softened

4 large eggs

Grated zest of 1 lemon

1/4 cup light rum

1 teaspoon vanilla extract

1/2 teaspoon salt

2 1/4 cups white flour

1 tablespoon baking powder

1/2 cup warm milk

1/3 cup semisweet chocolate chips (I use Guittard), whirled in a blender or food processor about 20 to 30 seconds, until chopped fine

Preheat the oven to 350°F.

Warm the cocoa, milk, and 3/4 cup sugar together to dissolve the cocoa and sugar. Set aside.

Using an electric mixer, beat together the butter and the remaining sugar until light and fluffy, about 3 minutes. Add the eggs, one at a time, beating after each addition, followed by the lemon zest, rum, vanilla, and salt. The mixture may look curdled at this point.

Sift the flour and baking powder together and, with a rubber spatula, quickly stir into the egg mixture, in three batches, alternating with the 1/2 cup warm milk, beating *only enough* to combine after each addition. Please do not overbeat the batter or the cake will be tough.

Divide the batter and add the cocoa mixture to one-third, along with the chocolate chips, stirring just enough to combine.

Fill a buttered and floured 9- by 5-inch loaf pan with three alternating layers of the two batters, starting and ending with the white. Use a knife to swirl the batters together. Resist overblending. I make a wide W to create a marbled effect.

Bake for 75 to 80 minutes, until the cake tests done. Cool on a rack for 10 minutes, then gently unmold the cake. Let cool for at least 1 hour, or even better, overnight, before cutting. A serrated knife works best.

Anne Fox's Fabulous Pumpkin Pie

Makes 1 pie that serves 8

A slice of this pie at the end of Thanksgiving dinner, and one for breakfast the next morning, collectively define Thanksgiving for me. Without both, I feel thoroughly cheated for the next 12 months.

1 (15-ounce) can pumpkin

3/4 cup brown sugar

1/2 teaspoon salt

1 1/4 teaspoons cinnamon

1/2 teaspoon nutmeg

1/4 teaspoon mace

1/4 teaspoon allspice

1/4 teaspoon cloves

3/4 teaspoon powdered ginger

2 large eggs, beaten

1 tablespoon dark rum

1 1/2 tablespoons dark molasses

1 3/4 cups evaporated milk or half-and-half

1 prebaked Pie Crust (page176), cooled

Preheat the oven to 350°F.

Mix together all the ingredients. Pour into the cooled crust. Bake for 45 to 50 minutes, until mixture is set. You can test by inserting a knife into the center. The knife will come out clean when the pie is done. Cool and serve with brandied and lightly sweetened whipped cream.

A Universal Rule

Your recipe is only as good as your ingredients. Don't stint when it comes to buying the real thing: full-flavored real chocolate, for example, rather than a chocolate-flavored preparation. You will know the difference and, since you put in the same amount of time whether you use real vanilla or imitation vanilla, I would advise you to use the finest available and make the time spent worthwhile.

Mom's Almost-Unbearably-Delicious Chocolate Fudge

Makes 1 serving for those who regard a 9- by 9-inch slab as a single serving

Now here's a recipe with almost nothing in it that is good for you; no oat bran, no yogurt. That being the case, it has an obligation to taste as good as it possibly can.

If you do not already eat fudge in the morning, you are hereby granted permission to do so. Think of it as a very delicious cup of superb hot chocolate that has somehow cooled and congealed. If you're not ready to eat it straight, you might want to crumble it into either hot or cold cereal.

The recipe comes from my mom's highly esteemed collection. It was written in her unique style: illegible and unintelligible. Fortunately, she was at my side, interpreting as we went along. The faded index card stated: "Beat till thickens." So I'm beating and beating and beating and, finally, I ask her how long I am supposed to do this. She says, "Oh, for a long time; it could be 15 minutes more. Everybody knows that." And when it finally did begin to thicken, she cried, "Be careful! It can turn grainy any second." This hair-raising experience yielded *the* most delicious fudge. I think my directions are sufficiently clear so that I won't have to include the 1-800-call-mom-for-help number in the book after all.

The necessity to beat 15 minutes with a wooden spoon may seem onerous, but I strongly recommend doing it by hand, at least the first time, so that you can clearly observe the physical changes: The sheen disappears quickly, and the fudge "grabs" the spoon. Neither grainy nor sugary, it is dark and rich and smooth. I intentionally don't specify the kind of nut, because any kind will do, and each one—from the traditional walnuts and almonds to the exotic hazelnuts, Brazil nuts, and macadamias—gives this fudge a different personality. In the unlikely event that any is left over, it can be frozen.

3 cups white sugar

1 tablespoon gelatin

1 cup milk

1/2 cup light corn syrup

3 ounces unsweetened chocolate

1 1/4 cups butter

2 teaspoons vanilla extract

1 cup chopped toasted nuts
(any kind)

In a large pan, mix together the sugar and gelatin. Add the milk, corn syrup, chocolate, and butter. Cook to a soft ball stage, 236°F.

Pour into a large bowl. Cool for 15 minutes, add the vanilla, then beat like crazy with a wooden spoon until the fudge thickens. It could take 15 minutes. The glossy appearance on the surface will dull, and the fudge will thicken suddenly and grab the spoon. When this happens, quickly add the nuts while still stirring and pour into a lightly buttered 9-inch square pan. If you dawdle at this stage the fudge may turn grainy.

Cool, cut, and insert a piece in your mouth as quickly as you can.

Chocolate Sin

Makes one 8-inch springform pan

Chocolate Sin first made its appearance on the Cafe's dessert menu in the late 1970s. It is a variation of a recipe I came across in a magazine, the original name of which had nothing to do with anything biblical or wicked. But when I tasted the finished product, the attention-getting name popped into my mind and I knew both name and dessert would be irresistible.

1/2 pound semisweet chocolate (Guittard)

3/4 cup unsalted butter

2 large eggs

6 tablespoons white sugar

1/2 pound almonds or hazelnuts, coarsely chopped, toasted, and cooled

1/4 cup brandy or brewed coffee

1 package Carr's Wheatmeal biscuits, coarsely crushed

Butter an 8-inch springform pan and line with parchment or waxed paper; butter again.

Melt together chocolate and butter in a double boiler over low heat.

Meanwhile, beat eggs and sugar with an electric mixer for 2 minutes, until very light. Then add the still-hot chocolate-butter mixture and beat on high for another 2 minutes, until smooth and creamy. Stir in the nuts, brandy/coffee, and biscuits.

Pour into the prepared pan and refrigerate for at least 8 hours.

Unmold. Cut into thin wedges to serve. Add a dollop of whipped cream. Delightful with fresh or dried fruit.

Crema Catalana

Makes about 5 cups

When it comes to custard, I never get bored. This recipe is yet another Catalonian specialty from the late Joana Bryar-Matons.

3 large eggs

1 cup white sugar

1 tablespoon cornstarch

4 cups whole milk

Zest from 2 lemons (use a vegetable peeler and remove only the yellow part)

2 cinnamon sticks (be sure these are fresh and aromatic)

1 vanilla bean, split down the middle

Place the eggs, sugar, and cornstarch in a blender, add milk, and blend for 5 to 10 seconds.

Pour into a medium-sized pot, and add the lemon zest, cinnamon sticks, and vanilla bean. Stir constantly over medium heat about 10 minutes until thickened. When the foam disappears, pay close attention because the custard is done, or will be shortly.

Remove from the heat and pour through a sieve.

Scrape the inside of the vanilla bean and stir the seeds into the custard. Rinse the vanilla bean, let dry, and store for future use.

Refrigerate the custard and serve when chilled.

Clay's Almond Cake

Makes one 8-inch cake

The late Clay Wollard, hair stylist and pastry chef *par excellence*, gave me this recipe years ago, scribbled on the back of an old Beaujolais menu. When I finally got around to making it, I was delighted at how delicious it is and how well it keeps (if you can just stop people from eating it). Its moist, macaroon-like texture and flavor make it a perfect accompaniment to a cup of aromatic tea or coffee.

10 ounces almond paste
5 ounces unsalted butter, softened
3/4 cup white sugar
1/8 teaspoon salt
Zest of 1 orange
3 large eggs
1 tablespoon Grand Marnier
6 tablespoons flour
6 tablespoons cornstarch

Preheat the oven to 350°F.

Grease an 8-inch pan. With an electric mixer on medium, cream the almond paste and butter until light and fluffy, about 2 minutes. Add the sugar, salt, and orange zest, and beat for another 2 minutes. Add eggs and beat for 3 minutes more. Stir in Grand Marnier, then the flour and cornstarch, until combined. Turn into the prepared pan, smooth the top, and bake for about 35 to 40 minutes. Cover with foil if the top starts to brown excessively.

Remove from the oven and let cool on a rack for 15 minutes, then carefully turn out and let cool completely. Serve at room temperature.

To store, wrap well in plastic wrap. Can be refrigerated.

Ginger-Apple Crumb Torte

Makes 1 torte that serves 6

I am often asked where my food ideas come from. Many spring from memories of past dishes associated with good times, often with my family. When my sister and I were young, we made a Mother's Day dinner (a *Sunset* magazine meat loaf for the entrée), which concluded with a traditional Swedish cake made with breadcrumbs and applesauce. For some reason, that simple dessert has always stayed with me. I thought of gingersnaps for the crumb, and my sister suggested using the especially spicy Mi-Del brand.

2/3 cup unsalted butter, divided

2 2/3 cups (about 1 pound) Mi-Del gingersnap crumbs

1 tablespoon white sugar

2 1/2 cups unsweetened thick applesauce, preferably home-made

Vanilla Sauce (below)

Preheat the oven to 375°F.

In a nonstick pan, melt 1/2 cup of the butter over medium heat. Add the gingersnap crumbs and sugar and stir for 3 minutes, until the butter is absorbed and the crumbs lightly browned.

Butter a 1-quart mold with 2 teaspoons butter and cover the bottom with one-third of the crumbs, then half the applesauce. Continue alternating until the crumbs and sauce are used up, finishing with a top layer of crumbs (3 layers of crumbs and 2 of applesauce).

Dot with the remaining 2 tablespoons butter, cut into 1/4-inch bits, and bake for about 25 minutes. Remove and let cool on a rack for at least 4 hours before serving. Serve with chilled Vanilla Sauce.

Vanilla Sauce   **Makes about 2 1/4 cups**

1/4 cup sugar

1 tablespoon cornstarch

1/8 teaspoon salt

3 egg yolks

2 cups whole milk

1 teaspoon vanilla extract

Mix the sugar, cornstarch, and salt in a heavy saucepan.

Beat the yolks and milk together and pour into the saucepan, beating constantly with a whisk.

Cook over low heat until the sauce is smooth and thick, continuing to stir. Scrape sides and bottom with a rubber spatula. Do not let it boil.

Remove the pan from the heat and strain into a bowl; add vanilla and stir. Refrigerate until chilled, then serve.

DRINKS

Hot Chocolate
192

Mom's Cocoa Syrup
193

Mocha Whipped Cream
193

Kemper's Domestic Wet
194

Kemper's Wet & Wild
194

Rhubarb-Lemonade Fizz
195

Rhuby Cocktail
195

Rhubarb Syrup
195

Lemonade
196

Hot Chocolate

Makes 4 servings

We used to serve a great deal of hot chocolate in the restaurant, both with and without Mocha Whipped Cream (page 193). I think people would be astonished if they knew the quantities of certain items even a small restaurant needs to make. Cafe Beaujolais only had 55 chairs, and we used to make 5 gallons of hot chocolate at a time. Let's see, that would be about one and a half cups per chair!

3 tablespoons white sugar

6 tablespoons sweetened hot chocolate powder (I use Ghirardelli Sweet Ground Chocolate)

3 tablespoons unsweetened cocoa (I use Scharffen Berger)

4 cups milk

Place all the ingredients in a saucepan and whisk over medium heat until combined. Serve hot or cold. If you have a steamer, use it to make a creamy drink.

Mom's Cocoa Syrup

Makes about 3¹/₄ cups

The memory of this delicious chocolate milk from my childhood prompted this recipe, an adaptation of my mother's from about forty-five years ago. She and I fiddled with the ingredients until we had something that met the expectations of our taste buds today. I think the combination of the flavorings gives a Mexican twist, but my mom, a fiend for authenticity, will have nothing to do with *that*, hence the current name.

1 cup unsweetened cocoa
   (Scharffen Berger)

1¹/₂ cups white sugar

Pinch of salt

1 cup hot water

3 ounces chopped semisweet
   chocolate

1 teaspoon dry instant coffee

2 teaspoons vanilla extract

¹/₄ teaspoon cinnamon

In a saucepan, mix together the cocoa, sugar, salt, and water and bring to a boil, stirring constantly. Boil gently for 3 minutes.

Remove from the heat, add the chocolate and coffee, stir, and set aside until cool.

Add the remaining ingredients and refrigerate.

To make hot chocolate: Stir 1 heaping tablespoon of the syrup with 1 cup milk. Heat, and serve dusted with cinnamon. Also delicious served cold.

Mocha Whipped Cream

Makes about 2¹/₄ cups

For an intense mocha hit, add this to any chocolate or coffee drink, alcoholic or not.

1 cup heavy whipping cream

4 ounces (by weight) semisweet
   chocolate, chopped

4 teaspoons dry instant coffee

1 tablespoon white sugar

2 teaspoons vanilla extract

In a small pot over low heat, warm and whisk all the ingredients just until the chocolate is melted.

Transfer to another container and refrigerate until very cold, at least 4 hours. Whip before serving.

Kemper's Domestic Wet

Makes 4 servings

Michael Kemper, an artist who worked the cashier/espresso station, invented two refreshing drinks. The nonalcoholic Domestic Wet combines tart and sweet flavors with a bubbly fizz. Serve with a brightly colored straw and a sprig of fresh mint.

1²/3 cups grape juice

³/4 cup freshly squeezed grapefruit juice (ruby provides a colorful touch)

1¹/4 cups soda water

Mix the juices together, add the soda water, stir, and pour over ice-filled glasses. Serve immediately.

Kemper's Wet & Wild

Makes 4 servings

Uses the same flavors as the Domestic Wet, but added to still and sparkling wines. Offerings from Navarro Vineyards in Anderson Valley have long been a favorite of mine, and their grape juices and Gewürztraminer wine are particularly well suited for this drink. If unavailable, use a good-quality grape juice and a white wine that is not very dry.

1²/3 cups cold grape juice

¹/2 cup cold, freshly squeezed grapefruit juice (ruby preferred)

³/4 cup Gewürztraminer or other white wine

1¹/2 cups sparkling wine

Mix together juices and Gewürztraminer. Divide among the glasses, and top off with the sparkling wine. Serve immediately.

Rhubarb-Lemonade Fizz

Makes 2 servings

We served a lot of this on hot summer days. Well, we actually didn't have that many hot summer days on the north coast, so we served it on foggy summer days, on cold winter days, and whenever else we felt like it.

2 tablespoons Rhubarb Syrup (below)
²/₃ cup lemonade (see page 196)
Soda water

Combine the syrup and lemonade, and pour into 2 ice-filled glasses. Top with soda water and garnish with a mint sprig.

Rhuby Cocktail

1 tablespoon Rhubarb Syrup (below)
Sparkling wine

Pour syrup into a champagne glass and add a small amount of wine. Stir briefly and top off with more sparkling wine.

Rhubarb Syrup

Rhubarb syrup left over from making Rhubarb Glop (page 14)
Lemon juice

Bring syrup to a boil over medium heat. Skim the foam that rises to the top and reduce by one-third. Stir occasionally. Add lemon juice to taste. Be careful not to overcook or the syrup will caramelize and turn an unappetizing brown.

Lemonade

Nothing beats thirst-quenching lemonade—and we generated *a lot* of lemon juice at the restaurant. Lemon peel went into so many recipes, it wasn't uncommon to see three cases of "naked" lemons in the walk-in refrigerator. The juice was frozen and used as needed. Simple Syrup, common in restaurants and bars, is a handy thing to know about because it ensures your lemonade will have no undissolved sugar. It's good for iced tea for the same reason. Try a shot of this lemonade in tea over ice for a different flavor.

3/4 cup Simple Syrup (below)

1 3/4 cups home-squeezed lemon juice

3 1/2 cups water

Mix the ingredients together and serve over ice. Garnish with mint.

Simple Syrup

1 cup water

2 cups sugar

Mix water and sugar in a small pot. Bring to a boil and let cook, over medium-low heat, for 5 minutes without stirring. Remove from heat and let cool, then refrigerate. Keeps indefinitely.

INDEX

A

All-Bran cereal, 38–39
allspice berries, 12
Almond-filled Butter Cake, 181
Almond Filling, 181
Almond- or Chocolate-filled
    Coffee Cake, 57
almond paste, 188
almonds
    bread fillings with, 37
    cereals with, 6, 8
    desserts with, 186
    Mandelbrot, 36
    nut fillings, 50, 57, 181
    sandwiches with, 109
    toppings, 51
Alpbacher Gröstl, 158
Amberger, Anni, 24, 93
Andouille Omelette Filling, 86
anise seed, 12
Anne Fox's Fabulous Pumpkin
    Pie, 184
Apple Butter Bread Pudding, 171
apple juice, 13, 51
apples
    caramelized, 10
    muffins, 25
    omelettes with, 84
    pancakes, 75
    poached, 13
    raisin cake with, 58–59
    salads, 126, 127
    stuffed, 15
    stuffing, 73
applesauce
    caramelized, 10
    ginger and, 189
    muffins, 21
    omelettes with, 82
Applesauce-Raisin-Nut
    Muffins, 21
Apricot-Almond Filling, 55

Apricot-Pecan Caramel
    Shortbread, 180
apricots
    dried, 50, 55, 180
    sauce, 143
Ardaiz, Lorraine, 42
Artichoke & Prosciutto Strata,
    148
artichoke hearts, 94–95, 148
arugula, 109
asparagus soup, 111
autolysis, 43
avocados, in salads, 129

B

bacon
    cooking technique, 87
    omelettes with, 84, 87
    pancakes, 75
    pasta sauce with, 139
    rice flavored by, 151
Bacon & Goat Cheese
    Omelette Filling, 87
Baked Blintzes, 170
baking powder, proofing, 31
baking soda, proofing, 31
Banana-Pecan Pineapple Ice
    Cream Waffle Sundae,
    69–70, 71
bananas
    fried, 11
    sundaes with, 69–70
Basic Brioche Dough, 45
Basic Sweet Roll Dough, 30–31
basil
    pesto, 141
    strata with, 148
beans
    black, 153
    white, 94–95
Beaujolais Blend Herbs, 93, 97,
    124, 153, 160

beer, Posole, 112
beet greens, 87
bell peppers
    chili with, 153
    frittata, 90
    rice flavored with, 155
    salad with, 131
    sauces with, 140
    tofu scrambled with, 161
berries
    crêpes, 166–167
    pancakes, 65, 76
    preparation of, 22, 65
Berry-filled Custard Crêpes,
    166–167
Bill Brown's Five-Flour Brown
    Bread, 38–39
Binah, Rachel, 55
Birchard, John and Barbara, 8
Birchard Soaked Oats, 8
biscotti, 36
Biscuits
    cornmeal, 27
    shortcake, 168
Black Bean Chili, 96, 152, 153
Black & White Soufflé, 165
blueberries
    coffee cake, 51
    muffins, 22
    shortcake biscuits, 168–169
Blueberry Cream Cheese
    Coffee Cake, 51
Blue Cheese, Bacon, Apple &
    Walnut Omelette, 84, 85
bok choy filling, 87
botulism, 144
bran cereal, 18
brandy, 58–59, 186
Bran Muffins, 18
bread, 34, 43, 47
Breads
    brioche, 45
    cinnamon-raisin, 33

cinnamon rolls, 46
corn bread, 40
five-flour, 38–39
Mandelbrot, 36
Polish raisin, 42
poppy seed, 37
rolls, 30, 32
for toasting, 34
Breakfast Cookies, 26
broccoli, and tofu, 161
Brown, Bill, 38
Brown Sugar Thins, 177
Bryar-Matons, Joana, 90,
    94, 187
Buckwheat Crêpes with
    Spinach-Dill Scramble,
    78–79
buckwheat flour, 78–79
bulgur, 38–39
Bun Bun Noodles with Spicy
    Peanut Sauce, 150
Burton, David, 76
Burton, Hilde, 63, 76
Butter Cake Crust, 181
buttermilk
    coffee cake, 52, 53, 55
    corn bread, 40
    cornmeal biscuits, 27
    Crème Fraîche, 135
    muffins, 18, 19, 24
    pancakes with berries, 65
    scones, 44
butternut squash, 115–116

C

cabbage, 128
Cafe Beaujolais, 1, 2
Cakes. See Coffee Cakes
Calas, 178
Caramelized Applesauce, 10
caramels, yogurt with, 164
Caramel Sauce, 56

caraway seeds, 158
cardamom seeds, 12
Carroll, Michael, 46
carrots
  muffins, 25
  relish, 142
  scrambled with tofu, 161
Carr's Wheatmeal biscuits, 186
Catalan Omelette Cake (Pastel
  de Truita), 94–95
celery
  tofu scramble, 161
  Waldorf salad, 126
Cereals
  muesli, 6
  soaked oats, 8
chard, omelette filling with, 87
Cheerios cereal, 38–39
cheese
  blue, omelettes with, 84
  Cheddar
    chili with, 153
    corn bread pudding, 154
    crunchy fries, 124
    Huevos Rancheros, 96
    Ole Souffle, 99
    pesto, mushroom strata
      and, 149
  cream
    in blintzes, 170
    herbed, 135
  dry
    eggs with, 93
    frittatas, 90, 102
    omelette with, 83
    pasta salad with, 131
    pesto with, 141
    sausage sauce, 140
    spinach soufflé with, 97
  Fontina Val d'Aosta, 148
  Gorgonzola, 120
  Gruyère, 149
  Monterey Jack, 96, 153, 154
  Mozzarella, 106
  peppered Monterey Jack, 156
  Swiss, 120
Chenel, Laura, 87
Cherry Clafouti, 173
Cherry Omelette, 89
Chicken Liver Omelette
  Filling, 88
Chicken Stock, 110
Child, Julia, 153

chiles, jalapeño, 99, 141
China Moon Shanghai Rice, 151
chives
  in creamed cheese, 135
  savory stuffing with, 72
chocolate
  bread and, 47
  powder, 192
  semisweet, 165, 186, 194
  unsweetened, 185
  white, 165
chocolate chips
  cakes with, 183
  coffee cakes, 50, 54, 57
  muffins, 24
  pancakes, 73, 76
  scones with, 44
Chocolate Coffee Cake, 50
Chocolate Sin, 186
Chris's Butterscotch-Walnut
  Pie, 175
Chris's Waldorf Salad, 126
cilantro
  chili with, 153
  quesadillas with, 156
  in salsa, 141
Cindy's Cherry Chocolate-Chip
  Scones, 44
Cinnamon-Raisin Bread, 33
Cinnamon Rolls, 32
cinnamon sticks, 134, 187
Citrus Salad, 129
Clay's Almond Cake, 188
Clevenger, Geoff, 78
cloves
  poached with fruit, 12
  in sauce, 143
cobblers, 173
cocoa
  cocoa syrup, 194
  coffee cake with, 50
  Hot Chocolate, 192
  marble cake with, 183
  muffins with mocha and
    walnuts, 24
Cocolat, 1
coconut
  muffins, 25
  shredded in topping, 174
  waffles with, 68
coffee
  chocolate with, 186
  cocoa syrup with, 193

dried, 193
muffins, 18, 24
powdered, 50
Coffee Cakes
  almond or chocolate
    filled, 57
  blueberry, 51
  buttermilk with cinnamon,
    52, 53
  chocolate, 50
  yeasted, 55
  caramel and streusel, 56
  apple and raisin, 58–59
  yogurt, 54
Cold Fusion Soup, 117
compotes, apples and pears, 13
Cookies, Breakfast Cookies, 26
cooking repertoire, 116
corn
  creamed, 99
  scrambled with tofu, 161
Corn Bread, 40
cornmeal, 27, 40, 99
Cornmeal Biscuits on the
  Square, 27
corn tortillas, Huevos
  Rancheros, 96
cottage cheese
  pancakes, 62
  salad, 127
Cottage Cheese Pancakes, 62
Cranberry Sauce, 134
cream, heavy
  caramel sauce, 56
  Crème Fraîche, 135
  pasta sauce thickened with,
    138
  sauce thickened with, 140
  scones with, 41
  soufflés, 165
  in soup, 117
  walnut pie, 175
  whipped as a topping,
    168–169
  whipped with mocha, 194
  whipped, yeasted cakes
    with, 58–58
cream cheese
  berry custard crêpes with,
    167
  bread pudding with, 172
  coffee cake with, 51, 55
  herbed, 135

salad with, 127
in savory stuffing, 72
Cream Cheese & Jam Bread
  Pudding, 172
Creamy Mozzarella Sandwich,
  106
Creamy Polenta, 121
Creamy Tofu Dressing, 137
Crema Catalina, 187
Crème Fraîche, 135
crème fraîche
  buckwheat crêpes, 78–79
  egg pancakes with, 76
  served with cake, 58–59
Crêpes,
  berry-filled custard, 166–167
  buckwheat with spinach-
    dill scramble, 78–79
crêpes, fillings, 167
Crumble Topping, 174
Crunchy Fries Extravaganza,
  124, 125
Crunchy Country Fries, 122
cucumbers, 142
cumin seed, chili with, 153
currants
  baked in apples, 15
  rolls, 32
  salad, 126
  in sandwiches, 109
  scones, 41
Curried Fried Rice, 155
curry powder
  eggs with, 93
  fried rice with, 155
  tofu dressing with, 137
  yogurt dressing with, 145

D

Daly, Garnish, 155
Desserts
  Almond-filled Butter Cake,
    181
  Anne Fox's Fabulous
    Pumpkin Pie, 184
  Apple Butter Bread
    Pudding, 171
  Apricot-Pecan Caramel
    Shortbread, 180
  Baked Blintzes, 170
  Berry-filled Custard
    Crêpes, 166–167

Black & White Soufflé, 165
Brown Sugar Thins, 177
Calas, 178
Cherry Clafouti, 173
Chocolate Sin, 186
Chris's Butterscotch-
    Walnut Pie, 175
Clay's Almond Cake, 188
Cream Cheese & Jam
    Bread Pudding, 172
Crema Catalana, 187
Easy Homemade Yogurt:
    Plain, Chocolate &
    Caramel, 164
Ginger-Apple Crumb Torte,
    189
Ginger Shortbread, 179
Mom's Almost-Unbearably-
    Delicious Chocolate
    Fudge, 185
Mutti's Marble Cake, 183
Pie Crust, 176
Strawberry-Rhubarb Pie,
    174
Warm Berries & Peaches
    with Shortcake Biscuits
    & Whipped Cream,
    168–169
Dickerson, Heidi, 66
dill
    fried matzo, 101
    in savory stuffing, 72
    smoked salmon and, 108
    and spinach scramble, 78–79
    strata with artichokes,
        prosciutto and, 148
Dressings
    goat cheese, 145
    hazelnut oil, 144
    pesto, 133
    tofu, 137
    vinaigrette, 144
    walnut oil, 144
    yogurt-curry, 145
dried fruit, scones with, 44
Dried Tomato Spread, 134
Drinks
    Hot Chocolate, 192
    Kemper's Domestic Wet, 194
    Kemper's Wet & Wild, 194
    Lemonade, 196
    Mocha Whipped Cream, 193
    Mom's Cocoa Syrup, 193

Rhubarb-Lemonade Fizz,
    195
Dutch Apple & Bacon Pancakes,
    74, 75

E

Easy Homemade Yogurt: Plain,
    Chocolate & Caramel, 164
Egg & Onion Fried Matzo, aka
    Matzo Brei, 101
Egg Pancakes à la Hilde &
    David, 76
eggplant
    filling, 86
    sauce, 136
eggs
    fried matzo and, 101
    frittatas, 90, 91, 92, 102
    Huevos Rancheros, 96
    Ole Souffle, 99
    omelette cake, 94–95
    omelettes, 83, 84, 86, 89
    Persian, 93
    potato salad, French, 130
    Salzburger Nockerl, 100
    sandwiches, 107
    soufflés, 97, 165
Egg Salad Sandwich, 107
egg wash, 37, 41, 57
Emily's Northeastern
    Breakfast Treat, 9
The Emperor's Omelette, 82
Entrées
    Alpbacher Gröstl, 158
    Artichoke & Prosciutto
        Strata, 148
    Black Bean Chili, 153
    Bun Bun Noodles with
        Peanut Sauce, 150
    China Moon Shanghai
        Rice, 151
    Curried Fried Rice, 155
    Mango Quesadillas, 156
    Pesto, Mushroom & Cheese
Strata, 149
    Scrapple, 160
    Tex-Mex Corn Bread
        Pudding, 154
    Tofu Scramble, 161
    Turkey-Fried Hash, 159

F

fish, salmon, 108
flaxseed meal, 34
flax seeds, 6, 26, 62
Fox, Anne, 184
Fox, Emily, 9
Fox, Margaret, 1
French Toast, 72, 73, 77
Fried Bananas, 11
Frittatas
    Joana's, 90
    Mendocino, 102
    Merry Christmas, 92
    Noodle, 91
fruit, dried, Chocolate Coffee
        Cake, 50
fruits
    apple butter, 171
    apricots, 143
    bananas, 11
    berries, 168–169
    blueberries, 22, 51
    cherries, 89, 173
    custard crêpes, 166–167
    dried, 6
    mangos, 156
    mixed, 20
    peaches, 168–169
    poached, 13
    rhubarb, 14, 174
    shortbread, 180
    soup with, 117
    strawberries, 174
    tropical, 68
    See also Margaret's Muesli;
        specific fruits

G

garbanzo beans, 113
ginger
    apricot sauce, 143
    baked apples, 15
    broth, 116
    muffins, 14, 20
    pancakes, 63, 64
    pumpkin pie, 184
    shortbread, 179
Ginger-Apple Crumb Torte, 189
Gingered Butter, 64
Gingered Vegetable Broth—the
    quick way, 116

Ginger Shortbread, 179
goat cheese
    crêpes, 78–79
    dressing, 145
    frittata, 102
    herbed cream cheese, 135
    omelette filling, 87
    pasta sauce, 139
    strata, 148
    stuffing, 72
Goat Cheese Dressing, 145
Goat Cheese Pasta Sauce, 139
Gramma Carroll's Cinnamon
    Rolls, 46–47
Grandma Kump's Asparagus,
    Tarragon & Garlic Soup,
    111
Grand Marnier
    Clay's Almond Cake, 188
    Trou Pain Perdu, 77
granola, Bill Brown's Five-
    Flour Brown Bread, 38–39
grapefruit
    Citrus Salad, 129
    Kemper's Domestic Wet, 194
    Kemper's Wet & Wild, 194
grape juice
    Kemper's Domestic Wet, 194
    Kemper's Wet & Wild, 194
Grape-Nuts cereal
    Bill Brown's Five-Flour
        Brown Bread, 38–39
    Breakfast Cookies, 26
Great Chefs of France Cooking
    School, 10, 129
green beans, Curried Fried
    Rice, 155
green chiles, Merry Christmas
    Frittata, 92
green peppers, Persian Eggs, 93
greens
    Bacon & Goat Cheese
        Omelette Filling, 87
    Smoked Turkey Salad
        Sandwich, 109
Grimes, Sarah, 40
Gritsch, Andrea, 120
Guérard, Michel, 129

H

half-and-half
    Anne Fox's Fabulous
        Pumpkin Pie, 184
    Artichoke & Prosciutto
        Strata, 148
    Cherry Clafouti, 173
ham, smoked
    Alpbacher Gröstle, 158
    Kasspatzl, 120
Harvest Market, 3
Haselnussbrot, 36
hash
    Alpbacher Gröstl, 158
    Turkey-Fried Hash, 159
hazelnut mayonnaise, 136
hazelnut oil, 144
hazelnuts
    Chocolate Sin, 186
    Mandelbrot, 36
    Margaret's Muesli, 6
    Nut Oil Mayonnaise, 136
    Poppy Seed Yeast Bread, 37
Heidi's Baked Sunday
    Pancake, 66
Herbed Cream Cheese, 135
Herb-Flavored Vinegar, 144
herbs
    cream cheese with, 135
    omelette with, 83
Hermann Loomis, Susan, 78
Holzrichter, Barbara, 56, 180
honey
    bread with, 34
    waffles with, 67
Hot Chocolate, 192
How to Repair Food (Bear), 39
Huevos Rancheros, 96

I, J

ingredients, purchasing, 184
jalapeño chiles, Ole Souffle, 99
jam, berry, 166–167, 172
jicama
    dressing with, 128
    relish with, 142
Joana's Frittata, 90
Jocelyn's Orange-Current
    Scones, 41

K

Kaiserschmarren (The
    Emperor's Omelette), 82
kale, omelette filling, 87
Kamstra Sugrue, Jocelyn, 40,
    41, 181
Kasspatzl, 120
Katz, Laura, 183
Keegstra, Beth, 148
Kemper, Michael, 195
Kemper's Domestic Wet, 194
Kemper's Wet & Wild, 194
Kent, Elsa, 183
kneading, 35
Kroninger, Stephanie, 100
Kump, Chris, 108, 111, 154, 174
Kump, Peter, 178

L

leeks, in omelette filling, 87
Lemonade, 196
lemon juice, Lemonade, 196
lemons, Pasta Salad, 131
LeNôtre, Gaston, 10
Leventhal, Michael, 101
limes, Orange-Lime
    Mayonnaise, 126
Lutge, Jude, 156

M

macadamia nuts, waffles
    with, 68
Madeira, omelette filling
    with, 88
Mandelbrot, 36
Mango Quesadillas, 156, *157*
mangos, 117, 156
maple syrup, grades of, 70
Margaret's Muesli, 6, 7
Margaret's Walking Salad, 127
marjoram, omelette filling
    with, 88
Martin, Leslie, 22
Matzo Brei, 101
Matzo crackers, 101
Mayonnaise
    Nut Oil Mayonnaise, 136
    Orange-Lime Mayonnaise,
    126

McCulloch, Janet, 38
Meats
    hash, 158
    prosciutto in strata, 148
    pasta sauce with, 139
    Kasspatzl, 120
    pork ribs, 112
    sausage in spicy sauce, 140
Mendocino, 1
Mendocino Frittata, 102, *103*
"mental" tasting, 6
Merry Christmas Frittata, 92
Mi-Del gingersnap crumbs, 189
milk
    evaporated, in pie, 184
    Hot Chocolate, 192
    milk powder, 26, 30, 34
mistakes, making, 39
Mitchell, Jill, 117
Mocha Walnut Wonder
    Muffins, 24
Mocha Whipped Cream, 193
Mohnkuchen, 37
Mohnstrudel, 37
molasses, Anne Fox's Fabulous
    Pumpkin Pie, 184
Mom's Almost-Unbearably-
    Delicious Chocolate
    Fudge, 185
Mom's Cocoa Syrup, 193
Mondavi Winery, 129
morning food
    described, *vi*
    genesis of, 2–3
Morning Glory Muffins, 25
Muffins
    Applesauce-Raisin-Nut
        Muffins, 21
    Bran Muffins, 18
    Mocha Walnut Wonder
        Muffins, 24
    Morning Glory Muffins, 25
    Name That Muffin, 20
    Oatmeal-Raisin Muffins, 19
    overmixing, 21
    Stinson Beach Blueberry
        Muffins, 22
Multi-purpose Apricot Sauce, 143
mushrooms
    artichokes and prosciutto
        with, 148
    country fries with, 124
    eggs with, 93

    fried rice with, 155
    frittata with, 90
    savory stuffing with, 72
    in strata, 149
Mutti's Marble Cake, *182, 183*

N

Name That Muffin, 20
Name Your Own Vegetable
    Soup
    See Grandma Kump's
        Asparagus, Tarragon &
        Garlic Soup
Noodle Frittata, 91
Nut Oil Mayonnaise, 136
nuts
    almonds, 36, 51
    chopped, 54, 55, 185
    hazelnuts, 36
    pecans, 25, 52, 180
    walnuts, 21, 24, 52

O

oat bran
    Birchard Soaked Oats, 8
    Bran Muffins, 18
Oatmeal-Raisin Muffins, 19
oats
    -based cereals, 6, 8
    muffins with raisins and, 19
    toasting, 6
O'Brien, Neil, 171
Ole Souffle, *98,* 99
Oma Leah's Potato Pancakes, 63
Omelettes
    andouille sausage filled, 86
    bacon & goat cheese filled, 87
    blue cheese, bacon, apples
        and walnut filled, 84
    Catalan Omelette Cake
        (Pastel de Truita), 94–95
    cherry filled, 89
    chicken liver, 88
    flipping, 86
    Kaiserschmarren, 82
    summertime, 83
Open-faced Smoked Salmon
    Sandwich, 108
orange juice
    coffee cake with, 55

relish with, 142
in Trou Pain Perdu, 77
Orange-Lime Mayonnaise, 126
oranges
citrus salad with, 129
cranberry sauce, 134
dressing, 128
Margaret's Walking Salad, 127
mayonnaise with lime and, 126
muffins with, 20
relish with, 142
scones with, 41

P

palacsinta, 167
Pamela Imbach's Famous French Potato Salad, 130
Pancakes
apple and bacon, 75
baked, 66
berry, 65
chocolate chips in, 73
with cottage cheese, 62
egg à la Hilde & David, 76
potato, 63
pumpkin and ginger, 64
pancetta, in rice, 151
panforte, 1
Panforte di Mendocino, 1
pannekoeken, 75
parsley, Pamela Imbach's Famous French Potato Salad, 130
pasta
frittata with, 91
pasta salad, 131
sauce with smoked turkey, 138
spicy peanut sauce for, 150
spicy sausage sauce for, 140
Pasta Salad, 131
Past-Its-Prime Poached Fruit à la Mom, 12
peaches, Warm Berries & Peaches with Shortcake Biscuits & Whipped Cream, 168–169
peanut butter
Breakfast Cookies, 26
Spicy Peanut Sauce, 150

pears
apples poached with, 13
hash with, 159
pecans
Apricot-Pecan Caramel Shortbread, 180
Banana-Pecan Pineapple Ice Cream Waffle Sundae, 69–70
Buttermilk-Cinnamon Coffee Cake, 52
Morning Glory Muffins, 25
peppers
jalapeño, in corn pudding, 154
pasilla, Posole, 112
red, scrambled with tofu, 161
Persian Eggs, 93
Pesto, 141
Pesto, Mushroom & Cheese Strata, 149
Pico de Gallo Relish, 142
Pie Crust, 176
pineapples, Chunky Pineapple Sauce, 70
pine nuts
omelette filling with, 86
pasta salad with, 131
pasta sauce with, 139
pesto with, 141
Poached Apples & Pears with Crème Fraîche, 13
Poached Fruit Mélange. *See* Past-Its-Prime Poached Fruit à la Mom
polenta, 121, 160
Polish Raisin Bread, 42–43
poppy seeds
muffins with, 20
bread with, 37
Poppy Seed Yeast Bread, 37
pork ribs, Posole, 112
port, Chicken Liver Omelette Filling, 88
Posole, 112
potatoes
Alpbacher Gröstl, 158
country fries, 122, 123
frittata with, 102
hash with, 159
omelette cake with, 94–95
potato pancakes, 63

potato salad, 130
scrambled with tofu, 161
Prune-Pecan Filling, 55
prunes, dried, Rachel's Version of the Anchorage Petroleum Wives' Club Coffee Cake, 55
pumpkin muffins, 20
pumpkin pancakes, 64
pumpkin pie, 184

R

Rachel's Version of the Anchorage Petroleum Wives' Club Coffee Cake, 55
raisins, 19
apple yeasted cake, 58–59
bread with, 38–39
breakfast cookies with, 26
cinnamon bread and, 33
cinnamon rolls with, 32
Kaiserschmarren, 82
Margaret's Walking Salad, 127
muffins with, 25
muffins with applesauce, nuts, and, 21
oats soaked with, 8
Polish bread with, 42–43
raspberries
coffee cake with blueberry cream cheese and, 51
soup with, 117
with peaches and shortcake biscuits, 168–169
raspberry eau-de-vie, 168–169
Red & Green Coleslaw with Orange Dressing, 128
red peppers, frittata with, 92, 102
Reinhart, Cindy and Charles, 44
relishes
Pico de Gallo Relish, 142
Rhubarb Glop, 14
Reuther, Linda, 115
Reynolds, Robert, 77
Rhubarb Glop, 14
Rhubarb Syrup, 196
rhubarb and strawberry pie, 174
Rhubarb-Lemonade Fizz, 195

Rhubarb Syrup, 195
Rhuby Cocktail, 195
Rice, 67, 151, 155, 178
ricotta cheese
walking salad with, 127
stuffing with, 73
spinach soufflé with, 97
Roasted Butternut Squash Soup, *114,* 115–116
Robert Mondavi Winery, 10
rum
apricot sauce with, 143
marble cake with, 183
pie with, 184
omelettes with, 82
rye flour, 38–39

S

saffron, eggs with, 93
sage
omelette filling with, 88
soup with roasted butternut squash and, 115–116
sausage, 160
Sage Sausage, 160
salad dressings
Basic Vinaigrette, 144
Goat Cheese Dressing, 145
Hazelnut or Walnut Oil Dressing, 144
Herb-Flavored Vinegar, 144
Yogurt-Curry Dressing, 145
salmon, 108
salsa, in Huevos Rancheros, 96
salt, types of, 127
Salzburger Nockerl, 100
Sandwiches
Creamy Mozzarella Sandwich, 106
Egg Salad Sandwich, 107
Open-faced Smoked Salmon Sandwich, 108
Smoked Turkey Salad Sandwich, 109
sap, maple, 9
Sauces
apricot, 143
cranberry, 134
goat cheese, 139
pesto, 141
pineapple, 70
smoked turkey, 138

Sauces, *continued*
 spicy peanut, 150
 spicy sausage, 140
 tomato-eggplant, 136
Sausage
 chicken-apple, 15
 hash with, 159
 omelette filling with, 86
 rice with, 151
 Scrapple, 160
 spicy sauce, 140
Savory Country Fries, 123
Sax, Richard, 176
schnaps, 169
Schwartz, Naomi, 72
Scones
 cherries and chocolate
  chips, 44
 orange-currant, 41
Scrapple, 160
seven-grain flour, 38–39
shallots, 151
sherry, omelette filling with, 88
Shortcake Biscuits, 168
Shredded Wheat cereal, 38–39
Simple Syrup, 70, 197
Smoked Turkey Pasta Sauce,
 138
Smoked Turkey Salad
 Sandwich, 109
Soufflés
 about, 177
 Black & White Soufflé, 165
 Ole Souffle, 99
 Spinach Soufflé, 97
Soups
 Chicken Stock, 110
 Cold Fusion Soup, 117
 Grandma Kump's
  Asparagus, Tarragon &
  Garlic Soup, 111
 Posole, 112
 Roasted Butternut Squash
  Soup, 115–116
 Spinach & Mint Soup, 113
sour cream
 eggs, 96
 omelettes, 84, 87, 89
 waffles, 69–70
soy flour, Bill Brown's Five-
 Flour Brown Bread,
 38–39
spatzle makers, 120

spices
 apricot sauce with, 143
 muffins with, 12
 poached fruit with, 12
 soup with, 117
Spicy Sausage Sauce, 140
spinach
 eggs with, 78–79
 omelette filling, 87
 pasta sauce with, 138
 in Pastel de Truita, 94–95
 soufflés, 97
 soup with mint and, 113
Spinach & Mint Soup, 113, 1113
Spinach Soufflé, 97
Spreads, 134, 135, 136, 141
squash, butternut roasted
 soup, 115
Stinson Beach Blueberry
 Muffins, 22, *23*
Strawberry-Rhubarb Pie, 174
Streusel-Caramel Coffee Cake
 & Caramel Sauce, 56
Stuffing: Savory Version
 French Toast, 72
Stuffing: Sweet Version French
 Toast, 73
Sugar on Snow, 9
Summertime Omelette, 83
sunflower seeds, 38–39
Sunset Magazine, 34
syrups, 70

T

tarragon, 111, 129
Tex-Mex Corn Bread Pudding,
 154
thyme, in stuffing, 72
Toasting Bread, 34–35
tofu
 dressing, 137
 fried rice, 155
 scrambled with vegetables
  and chili, 161
 soup, 113
Tomato-Eggplant Sauce, 136
tomatoes
 crushed, 153
 dried, 106
 eggs with, 93
 frittatas, 90, 102
 muffin with, 20

omelette filling with, 86
 salsa, 141
 sauces, 136, 139
Toppings, 121
Tropical Waffles with
 Macadamia Nuts &
 Toasted Coconut, 68
Tropp, Barbara, 150, 151
Trou Pain Perdu, 77
turkey
 hash, 159
 pasta sauce, 138
 sandwich, 109

V

vanilla beans, Crema Catalana,
 187
vegetables
 artichokes, 148
 coleslaw, 128
 curried with fried rice, 155
 muffins with, 20, 25
 omelette, 83, 161
 potato pancakes, 63
 pumpkin, 184
 relish, 142
 spinach, 113
vermouth, in soup, 111
Very Berry Pancakes, 65

W

Waffles
 bananas, pecans and pineapple ice cream, 69–70
 nuts & coconut, 68
 whole-wheat & wild rice, 67
Walnut Oil Dressing, 144
walnuts
 cinnamon rolls with, 32
 coffee cakes, 52, 56
 egg salad with, 107
 mayonnaise, 136
 muesli, 6
 muffins, 21, 24
 omelettes, 84
 pie with butterscotch and,
  175
 salads, 126, 127
Warm Berries & Peaches with
 Shortcake Biscuits &
 Whipped Cream, 168–169

watercress, 109
Wentzel, Kathryn, 75
Wertheim Rosenfeld, Anne, 64
wheat germ
 breads with, 34, 38–39
 cookies with, 26
 muesli, 6
whipping cream, muffins with,
 22
white hominy, 112
whole-wheat flour, 34, 38–39
wine
 cocktails with, 196
 cranberry sauce with, 134
 crêpes with, 166–167
 juice with, 195
 poached fruit with, 12
 in sausage sauce, 140
 soups with, 117
Wing Hillesland, Elaine, 51
Wollard, Clay, 188
Women Chefs and
 Restaurateurs, 3
Wright, Roberta, 121

Y

yeast, proofing, 31
Yeasted Apple-Raisin Cake,
 58–59
yogurt
 cheese, 127
 coffee cake, 54
 dressing with, 145
 pancakes, 64
 waffles, 67, 68
Yogurt Coffee Cake, 54
Yogurt-Curry Dressing, 145

Z

zucchini
 fried rice with, 155
 muffins, 20
 omelette filling, 86
 tofu scrambled with, 161